The Measure
of a
Christian

Dr. Charles Vogan

Copyright 2007 Charles R Vogan Jr
All Rights Reserved

1 **2**

Scripture taken from the HOLY BIBLE,
NEW INTERNATIONAL VERSION,
Copyright © 1973, 1978, 1984 International Bible Society.
Used by permission of Zondervan Bible Publishers

ISBN 978-0-6151-4570-9

Ravenbrook Publishers

A Subsidiary of
Shenandoah Bible Ministries

www.shenbible.org

Cover – "Abraham sacrifices Isaac"
by Rembrandt (1635)

Contents

Preface	5
The True Convert	11
The Disciplined Christian Life	47
A Church for Christians	87
The Kingdom of God	97
An agent of change	120
The Family of God	147
Led by the Spirit	167
Time to take stock	189
The Fires of Affliction	197

Preface

It's distressing to see the state of the modern church.

Instead of one Church (as we all profess – we are the "body of Christ"), there are a million factions that won't have anything to do with each other. And they all claim to use the Bible to support what they're doing. It seems that nobody is agreed on what it *does* teach.

Christians, for the most part, aren't training for anything – although the Bible describes itself as a training manual. (2 Timothy 3:16)

Church services are little more than social gatherings. The leaders have to be salesmen and entertainers to amuse the members or they will lose them to the church down the street that outperforms them.

All the sins of the world are also in the church, and it's embarrassing to read about them in the local newspaper. Evidently all that hard work at preaching and teaching isn't changing people's hearts. People aren't being saved from their sin, they aren't learning anything about God, and they aren't getting along with each other. The church seems to have no impact on our wicked society; rather our society is dragging our churches down to its level.

What often passes for Christianity in our day isn't what the Bible describes it to be. It's made to be easy, fun, not demanding of your time, and in line with the world's priorities. I'm afraid that if the early church of the Apostles were transported in time to our own day, they wouldn't recognize their spiritual offspring. In fact, they would probably be appalled at the radical change for the worse.

Something happened between their day and ours. Certainly the pattern for Christianity is still there in the Bible, but evidently we're not paying any attention to it. Our culture is dictating what our church should look like.

The Bible alone is our standard for faith and practice. This isn't hard. A true Christian should be able to see the truth about his faith in God's Word and live by *that*. It actually boils down to a few simple principles. It's just that modern "Christians" have formed their churches and faith around our modern culture instead of the Bible's plain teaching. It's a problem of willfulness, not ignorance.

A true Christian is an act of God, one of God's special works. He is specially designed to live with one foot in another world. You can tell that someone is a true believer by the fact that he will live a certain way; he's following God's agenda for salvation. For example, these things are (or should be!) true of any Christian:

- He has met God – and walks in his presence.
- He is willing to change.
- He lives a disciplined spiritual life.
- He goes to church for the sake of the Mission.

It's possible, however – and too often true – that a Christian won't live like this. The world and its temptations often turn him aside into following a "Christianity" that doesn't save from sin. But God won't let him get away with disobedience. For the person who still claims to be a Christian and yet he doesn't "walk the talk," God will resort to Plan B – if he really is a child of God. The Lord will not hesitate to use harsh discipline on his disobedient children, and they had better not miss the point this time. The purpose of discipline is to get someone back on track with God's agenda and growing spiritually again. We've been saved *out* of this world, and one way or another the Lord is going to prepare us to live in a perfect world with him.

Our purpose here is to look at what the Bible describes the life of the true Christian to be. Certain things will be real to him; certain things will be of great importance to him. He will go to a church that will help him achieve his spiritual goal. He will not miss the point of God's discipline, but he will present himself willingly to God's "rod of punishment" to be corrected and changed to conform to God's standards. The measure of a Christian is that he takes God seriously in his life now, in everything he does, and is walking on that road to Heaven.

> All these people were still living by faith when they died. They did not receive the things promised; they only saw them and welcomed them from a distance. And they admitted that they were aliens and strangers on earth.
>
> People who say such things show that they are looking for a country of their own. If they had been thinking of the country they had left, they would have had opportunity to return. Instead, they were longing for a better country – a Heavenly one. Therefore God is not ashamed to be called their God, for he has prepared a city for them. (Hebrews 11:13-16)

The True Convert

What it takes to be a true Christian

Shock

Many will say to me on that day, 'Lord, Lord, did we not prophesy in your name, and in your name drive out demons and perform many miracles?' Then I will tell them plainly, 'I never knew you. Away from me, you evildoers!' (Matthew 7:22-23)

By all accounts, our world should be converted to Christianity by now. Statistics show that evangelists and churches have led millions and millions to the Lord, both in this country and overseas. If you would add up all those numbers, it should be close to the world's present population.

Statistics don't mean much, do they? It's easy to see that the world is still in darkness. Our own country is in deep darkness, and suffering the consequences. The vast sweep of "Christianity" hasn't had much effect on our nation, nor even in today's churches. In fact, the church – where the greatest victories should be evident – is filled with "converts" who don't measure up to the Bible's standards. We hear reports of "thousands" who were converted in a revival, but most of those "thousands" soon go right back into their sin – and back into the world.

They certainly aren't going to church! The statistics on that tell us that our churches are shrinking, not growing. Young people aren't darkening the church doors, which means little or no growth for churches. Millions, we read, are *leaving* the church because they can see through the shallow and hypocritical nature of modern ministries. Church programs do not come through as advertised, and people are tired of it.

All this means that many are using their own definition of "Christian" which doesn't square with reality. It has become way too easy to become a "Christian" in our day; they call it "easy-believism." The truth of it is that becoming a Christian is the most difficult thing a person will ever do. I'm not saying that God has required great things from you at first – a new convert realizes that Jesus has done it all for us. That's the heart of the Gospel message. I'm saying that nobody can become a Christian unless a few impossible things happen first. Humanly speaking, it will never happen – not if we can help it. A true Christian is a miracle from God.

Most of us tend to stick with conventional wisdom – what our surrounding culture tells us about how things should work. Our present church culture tells us that it's easy to become a Christian: just follow these steps (1-2-3-4) and you're in. But what if the Bible tells us otherwise? What if God told us that we have to follow a different sequence of steps to become a Christian? Now we have *two* authorities contradicting each other – church leaders, and God.

Church leaders don't always get this right. A lot of them received training for *not* believing the Bible, as strange as that may sound. Some of them have ulterior motives in the ministry – you will find the criminal class in the pulpit as well as in the pews. And some leaders simply don't know the Bible as well as they should. They have extremely busy schedules, and they don't always have the leisure to study the Bible for themselves. Their lessons, as a result, are a quick summary of what they read in other authors.

The end result is that the church may not be getting the truth about the Bible from its own leaders. The Bible is a complex book, and it requires careful handling if you're going to teach it. "Not many of you should presume to be teachers, my brothers, because you know that we who teach will be judged more strictly." (James 3:1) People's souls are at stake. One mistake and you can easily steer people the wrong direction; it happens all the time.

Then Judgment Day comes, and we find out we've been following man instead of God – to our everlasting dismay. Being a Christian is not what many of our leaders told us. Like the Pharisees, the "Christians" in this Matthew passage made up their own rules for Christianity, and now they're in trouble.

I know, you don't think this could happen to you. But as a matter of fact, most "Christians" *have* taken the wrong road. They think they're going to Heaven, but they aren't. They've either been deceived about this, or they're deceiving themselves. How do I know? On good authority! Jesus tells us that in this passage from Matthew.

Notice that he says that "*Many* will say to me." Please take him seriously; he ought to know what he's talking about – he's the Judge! Put his statement over today's churches like a graph and look at the picture. **Many** of these people who claim to be Christians are *not* Christians. That's his judgment of our present situation.

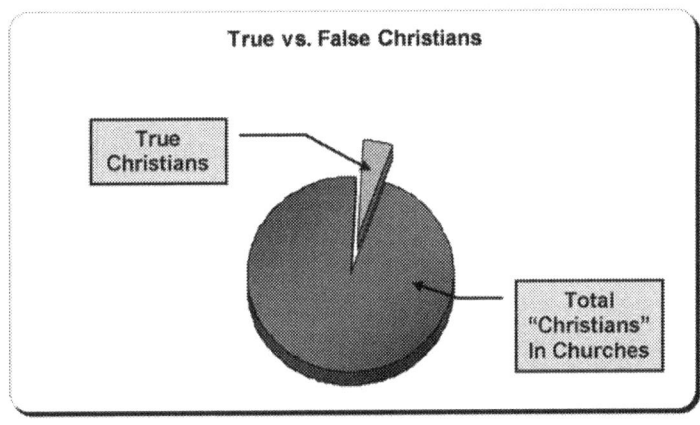

The True Convert

Oh, (*you might say*) but we're evangelical! The liberals claim to be Christians, but we all know that they can't be saved without the correct doctrine. We, however, believe the truth about Jesus. That's true, but correct doctrine isn't the only requirement for Christianity. There are a few things that the Bible tells us have to happen before we can truly call ourselves Christians. Unfortunately, these few things don't often happen in evangelical churches either. God's Spirit blows where he wills, and he doesn't work within the borders that we've drawn around ourselves. Our modern church has created a "new Gospel" that doesn't square with the Bible. Our church age is actually producing very few true Christians.

Notice too that Jesus tells us here in Matthew that he *never knew* these so-called Christians. This reflects a thrilling yet sobering reality of Christian conversion: it takes you *and God* to make a Christian out of you. It doesn't happen just because you say you want to become one. Follow all the steps – do everything required of you – you are still not a Christian. God must do his miracle upon you before you can truly claim the name. And you, and everyone else, will know it when he does.

For example, a person who lives in our country can claim to be a citizen, and even be a vital part of the life of his community, but that doesn't mean he is a citizen yet. The country has to bestow that right upon him. In the same way, many people are saying the "right things" and following the procedures to become "Christians," but it's not happening. You can tell that God isn't in it – the Spirit of God, with his distinctive signs, isn't there.

The problem lies in the fact that man sets his own rules for membership in the church. People decide for themselves what they're going to do – what they're *willing* to do – to be a Christian, and by golly God better appreciate it by welcoming them! Maybe it's ignorance (the leaders may have misled them about this), or maybe it's rebellion (they just aren't going to do it

God's way), but the end result is catastrophic. Either way, Jesus isn't going to let them into Heaven.

Notice too in this passage from Matthew that these people genuinely thought they *were* Christians. They were surprised to find out that they weren't. Someone lied to them. They were deceived into thinking that they had everything taken care of. The lesson is that it doesn't matter how you *feel* about your spiritual standing. You – and I – can be convinced that we've done the right thing, *and yet we might be dead wrong*. It is fatal to base our confidence on our opinions and feelings. Only a fool proceeds on that basis. A wise man will find out from God (and not go by his own feelings and opinions) whether he measures up to the standards. The Enemy would love for you to not check on this!

Fourth, notice from this Matthew passage that many people in this world aren't going to change. They will spend their lives doing their religion "their way," never thinking that something might be wrong with them. So, our warning will fall on many deaf ears. It won't do any good to show them this alarming trend in today's churches. God himself, as the Scriptures tell us, will close their ears to the truth and keep them away from the Tree of Life.

> Make the heart of this people calloused; make their ears dull and close their eyes. Otherwise they might see with their eyes, hear with their ears, understand with their hearts, and turn and be healed. (Isaiah 6:10)

As much as we'd like to see everyone checking on their spiritual state to see whether they are in fact Christians, they won't. As much as we make this truth easy to understand, people won't even think about it. Even if we paint this scene from Judgment Day in alarming colors, people will take no notice of it. This too proves, beyond all doubt, that to become a true Christian requires the hand of God – not my teaching, nor the will of would-be converts, can change a sinner into a child of God. That's why there are so few of them around – because man is trying to do this without God; he's ignoring the hand of God who alone can make a Christian.

This means then that, as you look around you in the church, you are seeing a lot of so-called Christians who really aren't Christians. They're fooling you. Not that *you're* going to be able to tell right off! On the one hand, it's not a good idea to try to judge others – you can't see into their hearts as God can. You're probably going to make a bad mistake about some poor struggling soul if you pass judgment against him and accuse him of being a hypocrite. On the other hand, you're not obligated to accept someone's testimony of themselves when you see pretty clear signs to the contrary. "By their fruits you will know them." If they hurt others, destroy the church, live in immorality, carry themselves in pride and arrogance – then it becomes obvious that they haven't changed any, which is the whole point of becoming a Christian.

In a way, becoming a Christian *is* very simple – because God does it for us. The work that we were required to do to reconcile with God, Jesus has done for us. There are only a few things left that have to happen in our minds and hearts to finish the work. But those few things are profound realities that completely change our outlook and life. It's the difference between night and day. One minute we are sinners in the dark, without hope; the next minute we find ourselves in an entirely new world with a completely different future ahead of us. It's like someone turning the light on in a dark room – now we can see what we were blind to before.

This difference that God works in us is what's missing from many "conversions" in our day. It never happened in these people. This is, in fact, the reality that Jesus will be looking for on Judgment Day. In this Matthew passage, he is turning away people who don't have plain evidence of this difference – whether they claim to be Christian or not. The mark of God's work is easy to see if it's really there.

Perhaps you can see now why it's so important to check with your Maker to confirm your "conversion." Yet once again, our God is being merciful to us and telling us *now* how we can make sure about this. The story in Matthew shows us people who find out too late that they don't qualify. But *we* have this story now, don't we? Jesus is helping us ahead of time before it's too late. Even though many won't bother to check (Jesus tells us here that they won't), we still have that chance. If we don't check into it, we will be entirely without excuse on Judgment Day. Nobody will feel sorry for us for being such a fool for not taking advantage of God's mercy.

What does it take to be a Christian?

What is the minimum that has to happen before someone becomes a true Christian? For one thing, you don't have to memorize the entire Bible! You don't have to be an expert in Christian doctrine. You also don't have to achieve great things, or do a lot of works to impress God. These are roads that too many people take to try to find their way to God, yet they don't see that their chosen path can't get them to their goal. The right road was made plain and simple for us in Jesus.

On the other hand, the entire Bible answers this simple question. The more that you study it, the clearer you will see the road that leads to Heaven. Simple, yes – but as is true with all of God's works, it's a profound and unimaginably complex system that God has put together for us so that it *can* be simple. The first Creation, in all its vast complexity, supports our lives in such a way that we actually have very little to do to be comfortable and safe. The second creation is the same way: God does the hard part, and we enjoy the blessings.

Actually it boils down to one common denominator – conversion depends primarily on *what God does to you*. And we learn this truth too from the first creation. We are told in Genesis 1 that God started with nothing:

Now the earth was formless and empty. (Genesis 1:2)

He starts with the same kind of material when he works with us. He's about to call us into his spiritual light and life, and make us fit to live with him in Heaven. We have nothing in our makeup that is capable of such a life – we are physical, spiritually dead, rebels, bound in heart and mind to this world, and strangers to

God. We can't see him, we don't know him, we don't even like him! So God has to breathe his life into this creature of clay to make us into children of God. *It's this first step that God takes that is his part of the process.* Unless this happens, we can call ourselves Christians all we want but it's not true. Once it does happen, however, then we must follow through and do our part.

That is the key to this whole thing that, unfortunately, so many people don't understand. They're putting the cart in front of the horse. They're doing what they think they need to do to be a Christian without God having done his part first. Of course they end up doing the wrong things (when God does his part first, *then* it's plain to see what we have to do!) or nothing happens even when they do the right things (because they can't do God's part!).

Conversion (from our perspective, at any rate) is actually a short series of revelations from God. We suddenly see certain things that we didn't see before. It's a light from Heaven; God convinces us with truth aimed at the soul, which nobody could have done for us so completely. The mind of man will never see these spiritual truths until God reveals them to us. And when he does, we can't deny them any more than we can deny our own existence.

So what we're going to look at is a partnership between God and man. Both elements are critical for a true conversion. One without the other does not describe a true Christian.

> For we are God's workmanship, created in Christ Jesus to do good works, which God prepared in advance for us to do. (Ephesians 2:10)

> Continue to work out your salvation with fear and trembling, for it is God who works in you to will and to act according to his good purpose. (Philippians 2:12-13)

Time to take God seriously

And without faith it is impossible to please God, because anyone who comes to him must believe that he exists and that he rewards those who earnestly seek him.
(Hebrews 11:6)

If there's one common characteristic across the masses of humanity in this world, it's that they are not interested in God. At least not the God of the Bible. Most people worship some sort of god, but they are idols – gods that people dreamed up and created on their own. The God of the Bible is not an option for them. This attitude toward God ranges all the way from no interest to outright animosity. When you talk to them about God – the God of the Bible, that is – you will get different reactions. If they don't actually respond in anger and persecution, they will argue with you about what God is like – primarily because they don't want God to be like the Bible says he is. And this is true even in churches, where there are as many definitions of the true God as there are church members! It seems that very few people are interested in listening to the Bible's account of God. The God of the Bible forbids sin – which is the main reason they're not interested in him.

Then the change comes –
and God reveals himself to you.

Suddenly, like being in a dark room and someone turns the light on, God shows up in your life. He's there, in all his magnificent reality. He isn't a story anymore. What you thought was just a concept from a history book turns out to be a Person who has come to confront you and deal with you. This is what separates Christianity from all other religions of the world: a true Christian has met his God.

He persevered because *he saw him who is invisible*.
(Hebrews 11:27)

God makes us able to see him. He wakes up our dead spirits – resurrects them with life from Heaven – and, like a newborn baby, we are aware of God now.

The experience shakes us. Our whole world has suddenly changed. Our world without God meant that we did what we wanted, when we wanted – we lived to please ourselves. Now, suddenly, we discover that this is God's world, and we are part of his Kingdom. In fact, this physical world we live in exists only for his purposes and pleasure. He is the center of everything, and the entire universe is his servant.

We can't escape this God. Now we realize that, for all of our lives, we've been running away from this God, thinking that we could stay away from him. We know now that this is a foolish idea. We can no more get away from God and his continuous gaze upon us than an ant can escape from inside a glass jar.

> Where can I go from your Spirit? Where can I flee from your presence? If I go up to the heavens, you are there; if I make my bed in the depths, you are there. If I rise on the wings of the dawn, if I settle on the far side of the sea, even there your hand will guide me, your right hand will hold me fast. If I say, "Surely the darkness will hide me and the light become night around me," even the darkness will not be dark to you; the night will shine like the day, for darkness is as light to you. (Psalm 139:7-12)

God has been this close and I never knew it before now! He's been watching me the whole time. He knows me completely, and knows everything I've ever done. All my arguments against his existence, and all my pride against his rule over me, and all my foolish claims of how I've lived a life that would impress him on Judgment Day, die on my lips – when I see this God in his glory.

I have no other authority now. If he would command me, I have no choice but to obey him. I can see that now. I would heel like a dog to his command; I dare not do otherwise – just as the wind and the waves obeyed him. This is, in fact, what the "fear of the Lord" means. It means that he's the King, and his power and presence so overwhelm me that I must do as he bids – or die.

On the other hand, I also realize now just how close I was to being lost without him. For some reason known only to himself, God has come into my life and saved me from the common fate of humanity. Everyone else is rushing toward the brink of the grave like lemmings, falling into the darkness of death never to come out again – and if it weren't for God's direct intervention I would have been part of that. I have been singled out as one of the select few to come into God's presence and deal with him about my soul. The thought staggers me.

Who is this God who has revealed himself to me? The Bible tells me, but my experience of him confirms it. It's not just head knowledge anymore, but meeting the reality behind the words.

- **God is holy** – which means that he is the only one I really need. He is the only good in the world. He is the source of all power and wisdom. He is life itself. My soul will live only in his presence. There is only God for me now.

  Why have I been wasting my time on other things? I can see now that everything in this world is empty compared to God. It's as Ecclesiastes says, chasing after the wind. I've been spending my entire life on things that have nothing to do with my soul. It's God that I really need.

  What is more, I consider everything a loss compared to the surpassing greatness of knowing Christ Jesus my Lord, for whose sake I have lost all things. I consider them rubbish, that I may gain Christ and be found in him. (Philippians 3:8-9)

If I live the rest of my life seeking God, that would be too little time devoted to the greatest of pursuits. And how I multiply excuses for not seeking him! I can see now that all else is secondary in importance. There is nothing else that compares to God.

- **God is a Judge** – which means that he not only has the right but the ability to examine me in every way to see if I measure up to his standard – his Law.

My conscience testifies to me that I am a sinner before God. Everything he said about me in the Bible is true. God knows me better than I know myself.

I know he sees me; he misses nothing about me. It's no use to hide anymore. The Christian lays his life out before the throne of God hiding nothing but offering all to the Judge, without holding anything back. I am at his mercy now, and he will do with me whatever pleases him.

I can see now that it doesn't matter what I think about my spiritual performance; if I try to judge myself, I'll always get it wrong, because I use the wrong standards for "good" and "righteous." God is the Judge; I have to measure up to *his* standards. If I don't meet his standards (and they *are* impossibly high – not a single sin is allowed into his Heaven) then I'm lost – my excuses mean nothing to him.

But I don't want to hide anymore; I want to come into his light, and open my heart and life to him for his inspection. I hope for his mercy; I don't want to run away from him anymore.

- **God is opening the door to his world** – When God reveals himself to someone, this can only mean one thing. Whereas the rest of humanity is plunging into darkness without God, in my case he has come to rescue me. The knowledge of God is the first step to salvation; I'm on the way to Heaven now.

  That's the only reason he came to me. God doesn't make himself known to people so that they can gain more riches and treasure. He's not submitting himself to academic or philosophical discussions. He has come with news of salvation, a way of escape from the coming wrath against the wicked. He came to get me out of this world before he destroys it; he doesn't want to destroy me too.

  This is an amazing advantage that God's people now have open to them. To be saved, the line of communication has to be opened and the relationship with God started. Going into this door now becomes the main business of my life.

- **My duty is to walk before him** – He has become my life, my light, my all. There is nothing else in life more important now than dealing with God on a continual basis.

  People accuse Christians of being fanatics about religion. What they don't realize is that the Christian is like the planet Earth revolving around the sun.

Without the sun, Earth has no focal point, no power to move, no light to grow and thrive. Take the sun away and Earth will die and disintegrate. In the same way, I now see that without God I would fall apart too. I literally exist by the hand of God.

> In him all things hold together. (Colossians 1:17)

I must now order my entire life around God – or die. Far from fanaticism, this is the reality of all of God's Creation. Those who ignore God are going to die forever. The only reason other people don't believe this is because they have *rebelled* against God and will have nothing to do with him. But it's *not* normal to live in rebellion! They don't see it yet, but they are dead and falling apart already because they are trying to live without God. Only the Christian has been brought into God's presence and started the process of restoration to life, to our high calling in God's Kingdom. To truly live is to *know God*. (John 17:3)

The bottom line is this: when God appears to you, you are going to *change*. Your priorities will change, your way of living will change, your likes and dislikes will change, your associations in this world will change, your hopes and fears will change. You will not remain the same person. If you are not changed, you haven't yet met God. Coming into his presence is the first step to a new life; it *has* to happen to be a true Christian.

You are a sinner

> *"Woe to me!" I cried. "I am ruined! For I am a man of unclean lips, and I live among a people of unclean lips, and my eyes have seen the King, the LORD Almighty."*
> *(Isaiah 6:5)*

The second characteristic of a true Christian is that he realizes that he's a sinner.

Pride will be the downfall of the human race. It has successfully hardened the heart, and blinded the understanding, of every person in history. We have surrounded ourselves with so many treasures in this world, and none of it is of any importance to our souls. Though you are a king or president, a warrior or an academic, a street cleaner or school child – you will all appear empty-handed before God on Judgment Day because this world is of no worth to save you on that day. The *one thing* that we must take care of is **sin** – and that, unfortunately, is the very thing we don't want to admit in our pride.

First let's get the definition of sin. We have to clear this up, because everyone has his or her own definition of sin, and they usually pick out something that is easy enough for them to change or do without. Sin is not selfishness, though selfishness is sin. Sin is not an immoral life style, though living in immorality is sin. You have to understand the *basic principle* of sin before you can understand why each particular sin is so bad.

> Everyone who sins breaks the Law; in fact, ***sin is lawlessness***. (1 John 3:4)

Sin is rebellion against God's rule. It's not doing what God said to do – or, conversely, doing what God said not to do. It starts with God's Word. He's the authority, he is the King, his commands fill the universe and guide its operations. When we do not follow those commands, then we are *sinners*.

You can see now why it's important to start with the awareness of God. Once we see him, and realize that we've been cutting out the very heart of our existence by ignoring him, then we can see how we stand with him. We were made to serve him

– and that's precisely what we haven't been doing. We've been living our entire lives by our own will, not his. When he calls us to his throne for an accounting, we have nothing to say – and nothing to show him for our service.

You have to be careful here about this issue of sin. It's not what *we* think might be right and wrong. It's what God told us to do. His full statement of his will for us is in the Law of Moses, a collection of 613 laws that are found in the books of Genesis through Deuteronomy. It is very clearly laid out for us there, and none of us have the right to add to or take away from his published will. We were created to obey the Law of God. It is a simple matter to see if we have been doing his will: Judgment Day will consist of comparing our lives with that Law in the Bible.

I hope you can see the problem now. Most of us don't even know what's written in the Law! How in the world can we claim to be "righteous" – in line with God's Law – if we don't even know what it says?

Most people will admit to breaking a rule here and there in their lives. Most people have heard about the Ten Commandments, and they know whether they've lived up to them. But what only a true Christian knows is how profoundly he has broken God's Law in rebellion and pride. Everyone else is busy justifying themselves in some way; the Christian is horrified at what he has done to God.

We like to make excuses for our behavior. Even Hitler had excuses for the crimes he committed. We also like to blame something or someone else for what we did. Looking for a scapegoat to escape responsibility is one of the first things that sinners will do to avoid conviction. Look at what happens in almost all court cases: the accused will almost always plead "not guilty," even if everyone knows he did it, because he plans to use extenuating circumstances, a scapegoat, some excuse for explaining his behavior. He doesn't think he deserves punishment. He can't live with the thought that he might be as bad as the accuser says he is. This is the heart of an unrepentant sinner.

But a Christian is different. Along with God revealing himself to me, comes the deep conviction that I don't deserve a single thing from this God. The same light that showed me God in all of his glory, shows my heart for what it really is.

Then the change comes – and God shows you what you really are inside – a sinner.

Suddenly all my excuses are gone. When God convicts me as a sinner, a knowledge of despair and alarm comes over me – I have sinned against this holy God! I have been caught, with the stain of sin on my hands and in my heart and mind. I can't hide it. And there's nobody else I can blame, because I deliberately walked away from God, whatever the reason.

The person who cares nothing about God will care nothing about the state of his soul. He denies that he is the sinner that the Bible describes him to be. The true Christian, however, faces it and admits it. He is, as the Bible describes it, appalled at what he sees in his heart. The unbeliever never thinks about sin or what he has done, or is doing, that so offends God. The true Christian, however, brings it out into the open, confesses his guilt before God and man, and starts working on finding a cure.

A true sense of one's sinfulness before God will bring us to our knees in fear. Disgusted with ourselves, we will sit before God amazed that we have tried to live without God. How could I have done that to him? How can it be that I have returned rebellion and an independent attitude for his goodness and faithfulness? When God has only done good for me, and given me yet one more chance to make things right with him, I have flung his goodness into his face and gone my own way. That concept of what he has done to God shocks the true Christian, and reduces him to a trembling soul before the throne of God begging for mercy and forgiveness.

Of course there is also the shock of the idea of punishment. So many people think that God would never punish them – or at least not much. They think that you have to be really, really bad – like Hitler – to deserve Hell. But a Christian realizes that it's not the number of sins that you commit; it's the state of your heart. It's not only a matter of what you have *done*, but what you're *capable* of doing. A murderer can commit his crime in his heart just as well as with his hands. (Matthew 5:21-22) And the proof of just how abominable sin is in God's eyes is the punishment that he brought down on Christ's head who suffered for man's sin. Hell is, in the true Christian's eyes, a fitting punishment for such a sinner as he.

He also realizes now how dangerous the world is. The things of this world have been temptations to lead him away from God. His friends and even his family have been instrumental in leading him away from God. In fact, the world has been a major source of the trouble. Suddenly it becomes paramount to the Christian to start cutting ties with this world of darkness and rebellion, before he goes down in flames with the world when God comes in his wrath against it.

A true Christian doesn't avoid the Scriptures dealing with sin – he deliberately studies them so that he can deal with it. He comes to God desperate to solve this problem. Only God, through the Word and prayer, can show us our sin – and until he does, we will never be saved from it. We therefore make it our business in life to root it out and destroy it, before it destroys us.

> Test me, O LORD, and try me, examine my heart and my mind. (Psalm 26:2)

> Search me, O God, and know my heart; test me and know my anxious thoughts. See if there is any offensive way in me, and lead me in the way everlasting. (Psalm 139:23-24)

This awareness of our sinfulness comes by the hand of God – in the Bible, by means of his Spirit showing us. None of us understands the true depth of the Law; few of us are very impressed when we hear sermons against sinners. We think that the lesson may apply to our neighbor, but not to us. Little do we realize what we are spiritually! Our hearts, hidden away from our own eyes, stink in the nostrils of God with rebellion against him. Every action is stained with the desire to be free from God. Our minds and hearts are steeped with this world, not with him. Only the light from Heaven will show us our true nature. And when it does, the child of God is shocked at the sight.

> This is the verdict: Light has come into the world, but men loved darkness instead of light because their deeds were evil. Everyone who does evil hates the light, and will not come into the light for fear that his deeds will be exposed. But whoever lives by the truth comes into the light, so that it may be seen plainly that what he has done has been done through God. (John 3:19-21)

It's not just a matter of escaping punishment. So many people use conversion as an "insurance policy" to escape Hell. Nobody wants to be punished, and for that reason we have to take a "jailhouse repentance" with a grain of salt. Someone who only uses Christianity to escape God's wrath will, eventually, return to his sin.

The True Convert

It's what we've done against our God that so shakes us. Rarely will someone experience that kind of humility. It's God-given. It's like a wife going back to her husband, realizing that she could lose *him* if she doesn't make things right. This is, in fact, the very image that God uses in the Bible to describe his wayward people. He, like an offended husband, is threatening to leave. Where are the true Christians who are alarmed at what they have done to their Lover to make him so angry with them? It's true, there will be Hell to pay for those who don't repent. But only Christians realize the true loss here.

> Come near to God and he will come near to you. Wash your hands, you sinners, and purify your hearts, you double-minded. Grieve, mourn and wail. Change your laughter to mourning and your joy to gloom. Humble yourselves before the Lord, and he will lift you up. (James 4:8-10)

So, when God shows you what you really are, you are going to *change*. There won't be any more pride in you. You will walk humbly before God because you realize just how much of a sinner you are. This is the only reason Jesus came to earth – to save you from your sin. (Matthew 1:21) So, *your* first priority in life, too, will be to address this sin in your heart.

Nobody else is to blame; this is your problem, and you must deal with it or die. And it must be dealt with – as it is with God, so must it be with you – it is the most important issue of your life. Everything else is secondary. *You must be saved from your sin.* Like the saints of Scripture, the true Christian will be humbled at the sight of his corrupt soul. Now he realizes how important it is to be saved from sin.

Jesus is your salvation

If you do not believe that I am the one I claim to be, you will indeed die in your sins. (John 8:24)

Jesus has been, and continues to be, a confusing person to many people. He put aside his glory when he came to this world, which means that he didn't look like he did when he was with the Father in Heaven. If you want a good idea of what Jesus looks like as the Son of God, read the book of Revelation. Even his beloved disciple John fell down before him in fear at the sight.

But in this world, Jesus has been the object of scorn and misunderstanding. Multitudes have no interest in him, even after hearing the Gospel message. Other religions grudgingly recognize his ministry as the work of a wise and good man, but no more. Most of the Jews absolutely despise him. Christians – well, again we have the situation here that those who claim to be Christians don't have any idea of what Jesus really is for them.

It's true that Jesus wears many hats, and it can be confusing to try to reconstruct from the Bible all the aspects of the work of Christ. You don't have to know all about him before you can become a Christian. In fact, you only need to know three key ideas. But these ideas are crucial – fall short here, and you will be no better off than the pagan religions who have no share in Jesus.

The early church fought long and hard over these doctrines. Fortunately for us (or providentially – no doubt God made sure they came up with the truth!) the church made clear statements about Jesus that separated true believers from heretics. They knew that anybody who doesn't believe the *truth* about Jesus cannot be a Christian.

> Every spirit that acknowledges that Jesus Christ has come in the flesh is from God, but every spirit that

The True Convert

does not acknowledge Jesus is not from God. (1 John 4:2-3)

A true Christian is going to penetrate the fog surrounding Jesus that confuses everyone else. It will come in a flash to him, like light coming down from Heaven and transfiguring the Son of Man before his eyes. We will look here at three truths about Jesus that the Christian believes, but the describing takes longer than the believing does.

The ***first point*** to get about Jesus is that he is ***the Son of God***. Jesus is nothing less than God. He is full deity. He is not what we first thought he was; the difference between our original opinions of him and what we see now in faith is the difference between night and day.

> "But what about you?" he asked. "Who do you say I am?" Simon Peter answered, "You are the Christ, the Son of the living God." Jesus replied, "Blessed are you, Simon son of Jonah, for this was not revealed to you by man, but by my Father in Heaven." (Matthew 16:15-17)

We are not saying that Jesus is all there is to God; the Christian doctrine of the Trinity states that God is Father, Son, and Spirit – three persons in one. To fully describe God, you would have to talk about all three Persons. Yet this doesn't make three Gods, as some religions accuse Christians of worshiping. The mystery of the Trinity is just that – a truth that is beyond our ability to grasp or adequately explain.

What we are saying about Jesus is that he is not created, he existed before time, he himself is the Creator, and has all the qualities of God. Since we can't say that about any creature under Heaven without being blasphemous, looking at Jesus in this light is therefore claiming that he is nothing less than, and nothing other than, God himself.

The reason this is so important to believe is that *only God can help you.* If the story in the Bible of the Jews trying and failing to please God by following the Law doesn't convince you, surely your own pitiful efforts at being "good" will. If left to ourselves, we can never satisfy God's demands. The Law considers us to be sinners and rebels, and the Law demands blood. We are already doomed. If someone doesn't come and rescue us then we are all lost. The story of Jesus coming to rescue us – and pulling it off magnificently the first time around – is proof that we're dealing with Someone unique here. He may look like one of us, but he has the wisdom of God, the power of God, the holiness of God, the righteousness of God, and the glory of God. Nothing less than the firepower of Heaven was applied to solve our problem. The "arm of the Lord" was revealed to us in the Gospel accounts. Now I know who my Redeemer is – Jesus is my God, my salvation, my only hope.

The **<u>second thing</u>** that you must believe about Jesus is that this Son of God ***came into the flesh***. God became a man. He humbled himself, became one of us, and took our place.

> Who, being in very nature God, did not consider equality with God something to be grasped, but made himself nothing, taking the very nature of a servant, being made in human likeness. And being found in appearance as a man, he humbled himself and became obedient to death – even death on a cross! (Philippians 2:6-8)
>
> This is how you can recognize the Spirit of God: Every spirit that acknowledges that Jesus Christ has come in the flesh is from God, but every spirit that does not acknowledge Jesus is not from God. (1 John 4:2-3)

The True Convert

Some people will admit that Jesus was God; they have no problem with that, since he did the things that only God could do. What they have a problem with is that God would ever become a man. They say that it was just an appearance, a vision, a spiritual image that only looked like a man – because everyone knows that God can't be his own creation!

That's no good. Though it looks as if it maintains the glory and honor of God (by denying that Jesus would ever "dirty" himself with our physical nature), it actually takes away a key element to our salvation. The Law demanded that *a man* fulfill the Law. The problem is that only the Son of God could do this successfully; the history of mankind has shown conclusively that we sinners certainly can't! So Jesus had to come as a man and fulfill that Law. The justice of God would never accept anything less. God cannot, and will not, waive the requirements. We cannot meet them. So Jesus met those requirements in our place. Now *a man* has fulfilled the Law of God, as required.

> Do not think that I have come to abolish the Law or the Prophets; I have not come to abolish them but to fulfill them. (Matthew 5:17)

What did Jesus accomplish in that? The Law itself tells us:

> And if we are careful to obey all this Law before the LORD our God, as he has commanded us, that will be our righteousness. (Deuteronomy 6:25)

A man who fulfills the Law perfectly is accounted a perfect man, a righteous man – a man who will be given the inheritance of God. That was, in fact, the original idea from Creation.

> What is man that you are mindful of him, the son of man that you care for him? You made him a little lower than the heavenly beings and crowned him with

glory and honor. You made him ruler over the works of your hands; you put everything under his feet. (Psalm 8:4-6)

The other aspect of Jesus becoming one of us is that he suffered as a man for the sins of mankind. This too was a requirement of the Law and could not be set aside. Our suffering for our own sins doesn't get us anything but eternal misery. But when a perfect man willingly takes on the punishment of sinners, he removes that punishment from the backs of others. He is a substitute for them. Now they don't have to suffer for their sins; he did it for them. Again, Jesus had to become a man in order to do this, to satisfy the Law. A man had to die for man's sin, since man is the guilty party.

Hopefully you can see how important it is to believe that Jesus became a man – we have no salvation apart from this. He solved my problems completely in his own life as a man.

The ***third idea*** about Jesus that you must believe is that ***he has become your life.*** I hope you didn't think he was doing all of this for his own sake! God came into this world to rescue *you* and bring you into a new kind of life.

> God has chosen to make known among the Gentiles the glorious riches of this mystery, which is Christ in you, the hope of glory. (Colossians 1:27)

Jesus has done the impossible for you – God became a man to take your place in both fulfilling the Law for you and taking upon himself your punishment. Now, you are in a new position with God. Your relationship with him is the same that Jesus himself has.

- ***You are now forgiven, completely.*** God no longer treats you as a sinner; in God's eyes, you are righteous

– it's a gift that Jesus bought and gave you. God has put your sins away from you "as far as the east is from the west." The work of Christ on your behalf was so complete that you will never again experience separation from God on account of your sin, you will never taste that wrath that everyone else is going to suffer under because of their sin. The power of Christ's righteousness, his sacrifice, protects you and preserves you. And this legal standing is going to have a practical outcome. Over time, due to the Spirit of Christ now in you, you are going to actually *become* righteous as he changes your sinful nature to conform to his righteous nature. It's going to happen – because you have been *made one* with the Son of God.

- ***You are now a child of God, as Jesus is.*** This is the staggering reality that even the angels long to look into. He didn't save us just to be righteous; he intends to make us *one with him* – part of his very Body – so that we can live with him, at God's right hand, heirs of God and sons of God – as Jesus is God's Son. I know now that I'm on my way to Heaven to receive my inheritance from God.

At this point you don't have to understand how all this works, or how Jesus accomplished it. But the true Christian, at conversion, has suddenly seen that all this is true about Jesus. He turns a corner in his life, so to speak, and there is Jesus.

The change comes – and suddenly you realize who Jesus really is.

It's instinctive: you gravitate toward Christ now, and he lives in you. That's what you want, and you know that you need him. You live before God as one of his saints, hoping in him, serving him, trusting in his care. What a contrast to your former way of life!

> I have been crucified with Christ and I no longer live, but Christ lives in me. (Galatians 2:20)

For example, the true Christian prays on the basis of this new relationship with God.

> Therefore, brothers, since we have confidence to enter the Most Holy Place by the blood of Jesus, by a new and living way opened for us through the curtain, that is, his body, and since we have a great priest over the house of God, let us draw near to God with a sincere heart in full assurance of faith, having our hearts sprinkled to cleanse us from a guilty conscience and having our bodies washed with pure water. Let us hold unswervingly to the hope we profess, for he who promised is faithful. (Hebrews 10:19-23)

We *just know* that God wants us. We know that we have access to him now, the same access that Jesus himself has. We know that we can ask for, and expect, the treasures of Heaven as if they are ours. The Spirit testifies to us that God is our Father now, and we act accordingly in full faith and assurance. The new Christian may not be accomplished yet in his spiritual life, but he nevertheless is alive spiritually and draws close to God for life – like a newborn baby suckling at his mother's breast.

> For you did not receive a spirit that makes you a slave again to fear, but you received the Spirit of sonship. And by him we cry, "Abba, Father." The Spirit himself testifies with our spirit that we are God's children. Now if we are children, then we are heirs – heirs of God and co-heirs with Christ, if indeed we

share in his sufferings in order that we may also share in his glory. (Romans 8:15-17)

There's something else that the true Christian will immediately realize about Jesus – and this is crucial. *Jesus is in Heaven now*, with God his Father. Heaven is where the Christian is also headed; that's our home now. We do not belong in this world, any more than Jesus does. He left this world; he is sitting at God's right hand. And since we have become one with him, that's where we belong. We are aliens in this world, and strangers; we will be persecuted here, just as Jesus was, and we will suffer trials here, just as Jesus did. Our inheritance is spiritual, not physical. We are on a journey now from this world to the next. Jesus told us that he's coming back, but only to take us to Heaven to live with him *there*.

God *will* reveal these things to us about Jesus so that we can be truly saved. If he didn't, we could never live by faith in the Son of God, which is the secret to eternal life. Every true child of God knows these things.

These truths, in other words, are going to change us – they are designed to conform us into Christ's image. We have been placed upon the Rock, and we now have a Mission. Our hope is before us. We will learn a lot more along the way, to be sure; but what we now know will save our souls. Jesus has opened the door to life.

We live in God's presence now.

We can see that we are sinners, and we need saved.

We can see that Jesus is our life now.

A sure sign

A real conversion has fruit. Someone who is only faking a Christian conversion isn't going to change in the ways that God wants to see. It may satisfy most people, but it won't satisfy God.

A true conversion, for one thing, will consist in all three basic ingredients that we've covered so far. Let's start with the negative side. If God hasn't changed you so that you are aware of him now and walk in his presence, then you aren't really a Christian. If God didn't change you so that you know that you are a sinner, and that you desperately need a Savior, and you are working now on getting rid of your sin, then you aren't really a Christian. And if God hasn't changed you so that you see in Jesus (only in Jesus) exactly what you need spiritually to live with God, then you aren't really a Christian.

A true Christian is aware of God now, and taking him seriously in all of his life. A true Christian knows that he's a sinner; that's been the whole problem of his life, and now it's the top item on his daily agenda to fix. He doesn't want to offend his God anymore. A true Christian sees salvation in Christ alone – the God-man who has the power and authority to save him from his sin and bring him to Heaven to live with God. Anybody who has only one of these, or even two, is not a true Christian. Christ doesn't do his job half-way. Either all three essentials are in your heart, or your claim to being a Christian is fake. This is the rock-foundation of what it means to be a Christian.

Furthermore, we must remember that God is starting an ongoing process here with our salvation. The idea is to complete the job, not to lay a foundation and then leave it bare. If God has done these things for you, you can be sure that more is to follow.

There are going to be changes that will eventually become noticeable. I'm not saying that it would happen immediately, nor are they going to pop out full strength one day. Like the mustard seed, they will start out small – perhaps difficult to see at first – and then grow until they become a major part of your life. Somewhere along the line others will be able to see them too. If you are a true Christian with the right foundation, the following things will begin happening in your life – like fruit growing out from a live tree.

- *True Christians have different emotions now.* They love the things of God; they hate the emptiness and deceitfulness of this world; they love other believers of the same faith. They hate sin and what it has done to them and to others. They fear God now, in a good way – meaning that they are careful how they walk before him. These and other emotions are new to them; they feel the same way that God does about these things. As unbelievers they felt the exact opposite about these matters; but if they are headed for Heaven, the heart has to match the confession. They have to be made fit to live with God.

- *They are standing on the Rock.* God will not leave his children helpless in a dark and wicked world. He will be faithful to his people and give them what they need to survive spiritually, if not physically, when everyone else around them is perishing. They will find faith to follow Jesus, in his light, wherever he leads them – even to the cross if need be. They will not be shaken from their faith and hope even when they lose this world's comforts. They truly are citizens of Heaven, and will find it easier to turn away from this world and its changing, shallow promises than the wicked can.

- *They have a high calling.* A true child of God has been lifted up to a high calling: priests and rulers in God's kingdom. Now they aren't living just for themselves; they are working for God's glory (by helping to extend Christ's Kingdom on earth) and their fellow Christians' well-being. They find the wisdom needed to do their duties; they find the courage and strength to stand in the gap in battle; they find the love for others to be ministers of God's grace to them. In other words, they grow up. They mature into Christ, and work as he does, in his spiritual Kingdom.

There are other signs too that prove that spiritual life really does exist in a person's heart. The point is that a true Christian will proceed along the way of life; he actually makes progress in the critical areas that secure his hope in Heaven. A person who isn't a true Christian didn't get the essential three steps, and so he doesn't change in the ways that God expects of him.

And we, who with unveiled faces all reflect the Lord's glory, are being transformed into his likeness with ever-increasing glory, which comes from the Lord, who is the Spirit. (2 Corinthians 3:18)

Remember, though, you can't simply apply these standards against someone's life and immediately judge him. A person may very well be a Christian and yet you might not see these vital signs in him. Who knows where he is on his spiritual journey? We are called to be charitable to others. But the point is that at some point these signs *are* going to show up. It takes time, but the tree will eventually put forth leaves and bear fruit. A Christian won't prove to be spiritually dead in the end, and an unbeliever will never show signs of spiritual life. A tree that doesn't bear fruit over time, or actually shows signs of death, not life, will be cut down.

A man had a fig tree, planted in his vineyard, and he went to look for fruit on it, but did not find any. So he said to the man who took care of the vineyard, "For three years now I've been coming to look for fruit on this fig tree and haven't found any. Cut it down! Why should it use up the soil?" "Sir," the man replied, "leave it alone for one more year, and I'll dig around it and fertilize it. If it bears fruit next year, fine! If not, then cut it down." (Luke 13:6-9)

And so God waits on us. If we take so long to change that we end up before the throne of Christ still dead, even though we claim to be Christians, he will (as the passage in Matthew 7 indicates) disown us and throw us out. If we show up actually changed from our former selves – saved from sin and made fit to live with God in Heaven – then he will welcome us in.

The True Convert

The Disciplined Christian Life

The Disciplined Christian Life

Whoever loves discipline loves knowledge, but he who hates correction is stupid. (Proverbs 12:1)

It's strange, the way people look at discipline. They accept it in many areas of life, even in sports and clubs, and yet they reject discipline in other areas where it's really needed. For example, the military runs on discipline – it can't achieve its goals without it. Businesses have some form of discipline among the employees to make a profit. Parents train their children and correct their wayward behavior.

Yet when most people go to church, they "let their hair down" and relax. The last thing they want to think about is any form of discipline. They just want someone else to do the work and they're going to sit there and enjoy the show.

Unfortunately they're missing the point of church. If your church is a one-man-show, it will do nothing for your soul. It's as if you are paying the preacher to eat for you – if you don't eat for yourself, you will die!

The point is that nobody else can make you a Christian – it's between you and God. The leaders in the church can only help you see what you need to do. But you also can't expect God to wave a magic wand over you and do the whole thing for you. There are many passages of Scripture that teach us our responsibilities before God. Until you take these responsibilities seriously, nothing will be done about the state of your soul.

What is discipline?

Discipline is getting yourself trained and in shape to do your work efficiently. Most of us aren't able to do skilled work right from the womb. It will take long hours of training, getting rid of the flab, changing our thought patterns, practice and practice, courage and determination. Paul uses the example of sports to illustrate this.

> Do you not know that in a race all the runners run, but only one gets the prize? Run in such a way as to get the prize. Everyone who competes in the games goes into strict training. They do it to get a crown that will not last; but we do it to get a crown that will last forever. Therefore I do not run like a man running aimlessly; I do not fight like a man beating the air. No, I beat my body and make it my slave so that after I have preached to others, I myself will not be disqualified for the prize. (1 Corinthians 9:24)

Evidently most people didn't know that they had to discipline themselves like this to live the Christian life. We all know that "salvation is of God," that we can do nothing to save ourselves. We have been told from the beginning that we have to trust in Christ completely to save us from sin and death. In other words, we mustn't attempt to do what only God can do. The unbelievers are trying to live a righteous life to buy their way into Heaven; we Christians know that such a thing can't be done – only Christ can pay our way into Heaven with his righteousness.

But while we have that part down, we tend to think that he'll take care of everything else too – without our help. The fact is, however, that he saved us so that we can get busy doing *our* part now.

> For we are God's workmanship, created in Christ Jesus to do good works, which God prepared in advance for us to do. (Ephesians 2:10)

> Therefore, my dear friends, as you have always obeyed – not only in my presence, but now much more in my absence – continue to work out your salvation with fear and trembling, for it is God who works in you to will and to act according to his good purpose. (Philippians 2:12-13)

There are some things that only God can do. But there are many things he expects us to do. For example, he's not going to tie our shoes in the morning! And if we're so foolish as to blame God when we trip over our untied shoelaces, he's not going to have any sympathy for us. In many ways we bring trouble upon ourselves because we're too lazy or unwilling to do what God has commanded us; and it doesn't help to blame him for not making our way plain if we haven't been obeying him. He has no intention of catering to our immaturity or willfulness.

> A man's own folly ruins his life, yet his heart rages against the LORD. (Proverbs 19:3)

But it's not a simple matter to carry out God's commands, not for us sinners at least. This will take discipline. *Discipline* is a way of life that gets the job done efficiently and effectively. It consists of:

- **Learning** – There is much for a new Christian to learn. For example, we have to learn about God – his nature, his expectations of us, his world, his works. Next we have to learn about ourselves: why we need God, why our lives don't work without him and why we're in the mess we're in now. We also have to learn about the solutions to our sin – the power and works that Christ applied to our souls, and the new relationship that he brought us into with God.

- **Being rebuked** – This doesn't go down well, but we may as well face it. We are sinners, willful and rebellious, and that is why things are so messed up in our lives. We *are* saved, but it's from the *power* of sin – unfortunately sin is still *present* and we are still too inclined to turn to our own ways instead of God's ways. If we really want to be saved from sin and death, we must willingly open our hearts to God and let him identify those sins that still lurk in our hearts and minds.

- **Being corrected** – Before a person is converted he lives his life exactly how he pleases. The problem is that this leads to his death! But when he is converted, the job of salvation is just begun. Now that God has his attention, he must instruct this former rebel in the way of life. These new ways of God are going to go against the grain – we aren't used to them, and we don't immediately like them – they don't cater to our fleshly lusts! But they are, like adjusting a ship's rudder, necessary corrections to our course. We may not understand why we need to follow God's strange ways, but that's why we have this new gift of faith – to enable us to trust Christ as he leads us to Heaven.

- **Training** – A life pleasing to God doesn't happen overnight. This is going to take some effort on your part. You will have to set aside time to work on this. You will have to submit yourself to training sessions, under the leadership of the elders who can help you get spiritually strong and skilled. In fact, it will take more time and effort than you currently think it will take – tough jobs like this always do. It has to be a cooperative effort between you, the rest of the church, and the leadership if it's going to work properly.

This life of discipline is, in fact, coming under the ministry of the Word of God – the special realm of the Church.

> All Scripture is God-breathed and is useful for *teaching, rebuking, correcting* and *training in righteousness*, so that the man of God may be thoroughly equipped for every good work. (2 Timothy 3:16-17)

This is what Church is for. If you have other goals in life that you want to accomplish, they are best done in schools, the political arena, the sports field, the financial world, etc. But if you want to be saved from your sin, delivered from death and Hell, made righteous, made fit to live with God, and have a home in Heaven forever, then the Church is the *only* place on earth to work on this. It would be a shame to waste your time, and the resources available to you, by coming to church only to watch someone else perform for your entertainment!

As soon as you walk into a church, you are giving yourself to the leaders to be taught and led. Discipline is the name of the game in a church. If you're not willing to do this, you are either a Pharisee – someone who refuses to learn and change, because they're perfect already! – or you think you're capable of running the show yourself, in which case you need to go start your own church. Either way, you're going to be a problem in that church if you stay.

Why is discipline difficult?

Some people will hear this and be filled with dismay. Why is Christianity so difficult? Why can't we just go to church and enjoy ourselves? Others are like the idealistic young man who signs up for military boot camp. About three weeks into training, he realizes that this is ten times harder than he thought it would be; it certainly isn't like the recruiters portrayed it! Why in the world is this so difficult?

Christian discipline is hard work for several reasons:

First, it gives us no sensual pleasure. Most people are all for doing things that make them feel good. But spiritual training doesn't stroke our five senses. We are called to live on a higher plane, to take delight in God and his spiritual world. But we prefer the "fleshpots of Egypt" to the desert life that God wants to lead us through.

Second, we are naturally lazy when it comes to spiritual matters. The sluggard's problem is that he feels no alarm, no crisis, no urgency to rouse himself and do anything. If we only knew how close we all are to eternity! If we could see the state of our souls as God sees them, we would be very alarmed and, with great energy, do whatever we had to do to avoid the coming catastrophe. But we don't see any of this; what we see is the peace and security of the comfortable lives we've built for ourselves.

Third, we prefer our sin to holiness. Discipline, after all, is designed to make us holy and pleasing to God. This will involve "crucifying" our sin, our very flesh and its desires. It will mean turning away from this world and its temptations to sin. We find ourselves very reluctant to put away our sin and live a righteous life.

Fourth, we are naturally rebellious against God. Just as every tooth has a root, this is the root problem behind every problem we have, including the lack of discipline. We don't want to follow God's will. We want to run our own lives, make our own decisions. Strangely, we would rather die than make any effort at all to submit to God and get our souls right with him. Even Christians suffer from this deep-rooted, life-long alienation from God. We are reluctant to pray, we find the holy life an embarrassment, we consider righteousness an imposition on our freedom, and we like taking a break from the rigors of Christian life whenever possible.

I only mention these things not to discourage you but to explain why in the world discipline proves to be so difficult. Perhaps the biggest reason that people give up on Christianity is because they weren't expecting it to be so much trouble. They thought it was going to be a bed of roses! After all, didn't Jesus die for us? Didn't he overcome the world? Didn't he promise to take care of us in all things? Why then are there still troubles for the Christian? Why doesn't God move mountains out of the way for us, and make the road level and smooth? Why are there still thorns in the path?

> The one who received the seed that fell on rocky places is the man who hears the Word and at once receives it with joy. But since he has no root, he lasts only a short time. When trouble or persecution comes because of the Word, he quickly falls away. The one who received the seed that fell among the thorns is the man who hears the Word, but the worries of this life and the deceitfulness of wealth choke it, making it unfruitful. (Matthew 13:20-22)

It's because the trouble is still in our hearts. Christ does, indeed, do all things well. But it's going to take some time to change us from sinners to saints. Not all miracles happen in seconds! The Spirit is going to apply the power of Heaven to break your sinful flesh of its bad habits and establish good ones – over the course of your life, in the midst of troubles and hardships. That's his way.

The purpose of discipline

The primary purpose of Christian discipline is to get you to listen to God for a change. This is because our fundamental problem is our rebellion against him. We have to start at the beginning if we're going to be successful Christians.

The first sin in the Bible describes the course of the entire human race. God told Adam and Eve what they were allowed to do and what they weren't allowed to do. Instead of doing what he commanded, however, they pulled away from God and started making their own decisions, based on their own standards, and following a course of action that suited themselves. It was life *without God*. And I don't mean simply that they didn't check in with him from time to time. Mankind was made to live in the presence of God, doing only his will, thinking only his thoughts, drinking only from the fountain of his life and power and wisdom, using only his Law and Word as the standard of what is right and wrong. When Adam and Eve turned away from that vital connection to God, they deliberately chose the way to death and destruction. We can no more live without God than a light bulb can work without electricity. This is, however, exactly what the whole world is trying to do. They do not seek God, they don't care about God, they steer away from God, they make their decisions apart from God. The result, as you can see, is chaos, disaster, death and destruction.

So the first order of business is to reconnect with God. Now at this point we have to be careful. Jesus is the only one who can reestablish that connection for us – *he* entered the Holy of Holies and reconciled us to God.

> Therefore, if anyone is in Christ, he is a new creation; the old has gone, the new has come! All this is from God, who reconciled us to himself through Christ and gave us the ministry of reconciliation: that God was reconciling the

The Disciplined Christian Life

world to himself in Christ, not counting men's sins against them. (2 Corinthians 5:17-19)

Now that the way to God is open for us, it's up to us to take advantage of this opportunity. But it's going to require crucifying this rebellious attitude we have against God and his will. He has called us, in Christ, to appear before his throne. He wants us to present ourselves for his service. He expects us to put away all other gods, to put the world behind us, to quit talking and start listening, to change and become like little children, to humble ourselves (in light of the embarrassing sin in our hearts and our poor track record in life), to open up empty hands to receive his Heavenly treasures of life. In other words, he's running this show now. It's time to bow down at his feet and profess him as our *Lord*.

I don't even know you, yet I know this is going to be difficult for you. We are so used to running our own lives that a change like this is going to be a long process, and painful to our pride, and a summary judgment against the pleasures of this world. It's going to mean a huge commitment on your part, a drastic change of life. This is, in fact, what keeps a vital church small in numbers – not many people are willing to change to this extent. But this is real Christianity.

The discipline of living in the presence of God means that several things are going to happen in your life. These are good for you – like eating spiritual vitamins.

- **You are going to become righteous** – *No discipline seems pleasant at the time, but painful. Later on, however, it produces a harvest of righteousness and peace for those who have been trained by it. (Hebrews 12:11)* This is the goal of all true Christians – the righteousness of Christ. The time for sin is over. Nothing else in life is as important as this is. At the end of life, at Judgment Day, the question to be answered for each one of us is whether we have, in fact, the righteousness of Christ covering our souls. Nothing else will matter. Without this we will never be acceptable to God.

In one sense this is the easiest thing in the world to do. All you have to do is trust in Christ as your Savior – he does the rest. There is nothing you could possibly offer God to buy this free gift, so you may as well accept it as a gift and be done with it.

In another sense, however, the battle is just begun when God gives us this righteousness. Now we have to start acting the part! It doesn't befit the righteous children of God to continue in their sin. "What then? Shall we sin because we are not under Law but under grace? By no means!" (Romans 6:15) You will find a righteous life to be a matter of severe discipline, but it leads to a life of peace and joy that your former ways could never do for you. The regimen of following Christ and living in him isn't going to feel good to the "old nature" in us that still wants to sin; but it's medicine for the soul.

- **You are going to be weaned from the world** – This world's days are numbered. When God first made the world, it was a good and beautiful place. But the partnership between man and Satan has turned the world into a spiritual wasteland, a deadly circus where we can fulfill our raging lusts through an assortment of appealing sideshows.

  The time has come to leave this world behind. We don't belong here, so let's cut our ties and prepare for the move to a better world. God has so much more in store for us than what this world has to offer – and it's all good, pure, beautiful, clean, wholesome, uplifting, holy, and centered on him.

The trouble is that it's not going to be easy to cut the ties to this world. It will require a Spartan view of life – crucifying the flesh that inclines so strongly toward satisfying its lusts at the world's fountains of pleasures. It will take persistence, courage, and strength – the power of Christ, as a matter of fact, who successfully turned away from this world and put it beneath his feet. Paul said it best.

> Brothers, I do not consider myself yet to have taken hold of it. But one thing I do: Forgetting what is behind and straining toward what is ahead, I press on toward the goal to win the prize for which God has called me Heavenward in Christ Jesus. (Philippians 3:13-14)

- **You will be trained for battle** – One of the worst things you could possibly do is go to war without first being trained. The military puts its recruits through severe discipline with no apologies, because this harsh training will save their lives on the battlefield. And well-trained soldiers win battles.

The church needs well-trained spiritual soldiers if she's going to win the battles against her enemies. Our three main enemies – the ***world*** and its temptations and perversions, the ***flesh*** with its inclination to sin and to taste the world's temptations, and the ***devil*** who deceives us into sin – are ruthless and deadly. They never let up, and they attack everyone, both unbeliever and Christian. Christ trains and arms God's people against these enemies, to the extent that we can never lose – if we follow his training.

The training has to be extensive, continuous, and to the point. The goal is that every Christian will know exactly what to do, when to do it, and follow through with what needs to be done without hesitation. This is, after all, war – and people die in war over the slightest misstep or hesitation. Since the enemy takes no prisoners, we can afford no mistakes. The discipline in the church will prepare us for this kind of action.

- **You will become more mature spiritually** – A child is just as much a member of the family as the parents, but he has little or no discipline yet and can't really help out much. An adult, however, is fully capable of taking care of matters of the household.

  The difference between disciplined and undisciplined Christians is found in this matter of maturity. An immature Christian does exactly what pleases him, he won't listen to those in authority over him, he refuses to be led, he helps nobody but himself, and is a general nuisance in the church – just like a bratty kid. A mature Christian, however, is thinking of the needs of others, of the needs of the church at large, the glory of God, the growth of Christ's kingdom. You don't have to tell him to pray for the saints because their spiritual needs are on his heart continually. Sin is repulsive to him. He understands the authority of Christ and following the will of Christ in the functions of the church.

It generally takes twenty years to raise a child to maturity. Christians, on the other hand, grow at different rates spiritually, but the point is the same – it requires time and work and discipline to change baby Christians to mature saints. Don't expect much out of the babies yet, but you should be alarmed when years of work haven't had any maturing effect on some pew-sitting Christian.

Disciplined to do what?

Most people are at least somewhat disciplined. We've learned how to get along with others to some extent, most of us aren't breaking the law, most of us have a job and many have families that we're responsible for. There has to be some degree of discipline in our lives just to get along from day to day.

But spiritually speaking, we all start out just as undisciplined as a new-born baby. The thing is that we don't usually know it – nor are we willing to admit it. And right there is the problem that most people have about submitting to discipline in the church – if they're already responsible citizens in society, why should the church consider them in need of *more* discipline?

Because the world of God is a new world. It isn't like this physical world. We may be very mature and disciplined in our jobs, community, family – but that doesn't carry over into the church. Here we are starting all over again. We have a new language to learn, new values to pick up, new friendships to make, new relationships with God and our spiritual family, a new position as Christians in a fallen and perverted world. That's why the successful in this world aren't necessarily (in fact, usually aren't!) successful spiritually. They have a real problem adjusting to the new world; they're still trying their old ways and opinions in the church and it doesn't work.

This is why Jesus told us that we must become like little children. Get rid of your adult pride, humble yourself before God and man, and *learn*. You have to get detoxified, so to speak, of all that you learned and picked up from this present world – it leads to death, not life. Your brain and heart have to be reprogrammed like a computer; the old programming is no good and absolutely useless in the church. You have to start at the beginning and learn a new way of living.

Therefore, rid yourselves of all malice and all deceit, hypocrisy, envy, and slander of every kind. Like newborn babies, crave pure spiritual milk, so that by it you may grow up in your salvation, now that you have tasted that the Lord is good. (1 Peter 2:1-3)

What are the areas that we need discipline in?

The Priorities – Jesus told us that the riches of this world are of no value in the Kingdom of God – only the treasures of Heaven are worth anything. The Bible is worth more than silver and gold, Proverbs tells us. Our brothers and sisters in the church are our family now, much more so than our physical families – who will too often make it difficult to live our Christian lives.

The Word – The Bible is the only truth, the only right way to look at things. We've been so filled with the lies and distortions of the Enemy that it's going to take a lot of study and work to get rid of our wrong notions and look at things the way God sees them. The Bible will give us everything we need to live as Christians; we dare not change or ignore any part of it.

Prayer – Talking to God isn't an easy matter. God is no fool, and he knows what's in our hearts. It's time to be honest and open with him. Prayer isn't simply presenting a "Christmas list" to God as if he were Santa

Claus. It's a matter of presenting our sinful hearts to him for his will and power to change. It's putting ourselves before his throne to receive what he has for us in Jesus. It's a time for listening, not talking; humbly receiving, not showing off; showing up to serve the King, not insisting that he fulfill our demands now.

Fellowship with the saints – Besides our broken relationship with God, our relationship with others is the most serious problem of life. We usually limit our time around other people to a short hour on Sunday morning; if we involve ourselves with them any more than this, we end up fighting, gossiping, causing trouble and dissention, and generally being nasty to others. It's going to require the power of the Spirit and the wisdom of God's Word to change us from nasty to nice – what Paul calls the "fruit of the Spirit."

The world doesn't teach these things. We don't inherit these skills or interests from our parents. The most experienced or street-savvy person in the world would feel helpless and bewildered in the midst of a spiritually active church. These things are matters of the Kingdom of God, and can only be learned and appreciated by dedicated citizens of Heaven.

Types of discipline

Your parents first taught you the way discipline works, if they were good parents doing their job. First, they told you what they wanted you to do, or they told you what not to do. Then, if you disobeyed them, they rebuked you for your crime. Finally, if you insisted on disobeying them by committing the crime again, the paddle came out and you learned the lesson through pain.

This is exactly how God disciplines his people. I call it "learning the easy way or learning the hard way." Unfortunately, most people end up learning the hard way – including in the church. So if God really cares about you, you're going to learn these lessons one way or another.

> *And you have forgotten that word of encouragement that addresses you as sons: "My son, do not make light of the Lord's discipline, and do not lose heart when he rebukes you, because the Lord disciplines those he loves, and he punishes everyone he accepts as a son." Endure hardship as discipline; God is treating you as sons. For what son is not disciplined by his father? (Hebrews 12:5-7)*

- **Through the Word and Spirit** – God in his mercy and grace gave us the *Bible* to show us the truth, and the *Spirit* to enlighten us to understand it and empower us to follow it. The Bible is the perfect description of what we need to know about God and his spiritual world. We need nothing more than the Bible, and we need the entire Bible. Here is the power behind the ministry of the church. Preaching and teaching the Word to God's saints is the primary method of getting them saved from sin and ready for Heaven. And the Spirit makes the world of the Bible real to them by opening their eyes and hearts to the reality of God.

  However, very few people take the Bible seriously. They know almost nothing about it, and they don't care that they don't. That's like a starving man looking at a full-course meal and turning his back on it! It makes no sense. And on Judgment Day such people will find out how stupid a thing that was, to casually turn away from the truth that would save them.

Some, however, jump at the chance to learn all that they can from the Word. They can see how precious this truth is. They draw near to God through his Word and find out how precious Jesus really is. They learn how to use it to solve the problems in their lives. You don't have to push these people to study the Bible – they are there in church every time it's taught, ready to learn all that they can. They meditate on the Word "day and night" in order to get it into their hearts and minds.

It's far better to learn the truth and put it into practice, right from the start. It gets you ready, trained, and open to God's leading. But I'm afraid that not many have this kind of foresight. In our society, there seem to be more enticing things to do besides studying the Bible. People like that are, unfortunately, going to lose the war.

- ***Through the Church*** – God also disciplines his people through the church's government. Many people don't have the interest to pursue spiritual matters on their own – they just come to church and let someone else do all the work for them. They're not really interested in changing; they come to church because they think that, just by showing up, that will make God pleased with them.

  The trouble is that at some point they're going to run into problems and not know what to do. It never dawned on them that they had to learn how to take care of themselves spiritually. This is where the elders step in. They have to take such people by the hand and lead them into the truth, sometimes firmly, so that their character flaws don't turn into a spiritual disaster. At times the form of discipline will be a rebuke about a sin that they're committing. At other times it will be praying for them, or confronting them with some pertinent Scripture, in an effort to change their thinking or behavior.

People like this have to be led, because they're not going to do it on their own. They need external discipline, a church government, overseers who make them see the need to change. Church isn't a religious club; it's the one opportunity in this world for change – from sinner to saint. But like children who won't do anything unless they are told to, many church-goers won't take any action on the plain truth of the Word until they are brought face to face with it through the church's system of discipline.

- **Through hardships and trials** – And then there are those who resist the truth with all their might. They have no intention of changing. The Word makes no impression on them, they aren't in church to change anything about themselves, and they resent any interference from church leaders. They want to run their own lives. When these people start making trouble in the church – and they will, eventually! – it's time to turn them out to learn their lessons the hard way. The church doesn't need troublemakers in its midst. Another way that the church will be free of them (in fact, what most often happens in our modern society) is that they'll leave in a huff on their own over some pretext of being insulted or mistreated.

Let them go. People like that will only learn by harsh punishment. God has a way of dealing with difficult people.

> I will instruct you and teach you in the way you should go; I will counsel you and watch over you. Do not be like the horse or the mule, which have no understanding but must be controlled by bit and bridle or they will not come to you. (Psalm 32:8-9)

The "bit and bridle" refers to wandering in spiritual wastelands with nothing to feed the soul, loss of Christian friends, getting tied down with materialism that dries up the soul, even catastrophes like loss of health or jobs, bankruptcy, etc. God has a lot of options available to him to teach harsh lessons to mule-headed people who won't learn the easy way. God will resort to stern methods that we didn't think he would do to his own children! Don't underestimate his determination to change you, one way or another.

And then there are those times when he brings hardship into the lives of his saints because it's really the best way (not necessarily because of their sin) to learn a lesson. Job found this out. He knew he didn't do anything to deserve such harsh treatment, but he learned something about God that he wouldn't have learned any other way.

> In this you greatly rejoice, though now for a little while you may have had to suffer grief in all kinds of trials. These have come so that your faith – of greater worth than gold, which perishes even though refined by fire – may be proved genuine and may result in praise, glory and honor when Jesus Christ is revealed. (1 Peter 1:6-7)

Again, don't make the mistake of thinking that God would never treat you with sternness. He will when he so chooses. The point is that he knows what he's doing. We pass the test when we accept *anything* that comes from his hand, both good times and bad.

> And we know that in all things God works for the good of those who love him, who have been called according to his purpose. (Romans 8:28)

Responding to discipline

Discipline is perhaps the hardest thing about church. I've seen more people fail over this than over any other issue. Usually most people will listen to the teaching and preaching. Most people will agree to the need (if they don't actually get up and do it!) for participation in the life of the church. But *most* people that I've encountered in the church refuse to be disciplined. They either think they don't need it, or it hurts their pride, or they feel the heat on their sinful lifestyle and attitude. In fact, 98% of the people who leave the church "offended" over some trivial issue are the ones who refused to submit to discipline.

Let's be plain here. It's true, we live in America where everyone can do exactly as they please as long as they aren't breaking one of the laws of the land. A person can go to whatever church they want, and they can leave when they want. But God said that a person who refuses to submit to discipline is a *fool*.

> The fear of the LORD is the beginning of knowledge, but fools despise wisdom and discipline. (Proverbs 1:7)

> He who ignores discipline comes to poverty and shame, but whoever heeds correction is honored. (Proverbs 13:18)

> Stern discipline awaits him who leaves the path; he who hates correction will die. (Proverbs 15:10)

The church ought to accept anybody who comes to worship God and grow spiritually – the doors are open to all who will come. But there are two kinds of people that the church *doesn't* need. ***First***, the church doesn't need Pharisees – the "experts" in religion who think they have no more room to improve. You can't teach them anything; they already know what they want to know, and they think they know as much as any pastor or teacher in the church. They aren't there to learn, they aren't there to change – they are there to show off what fine Christians they are.

> Do you see a man wise in his own eyes? There is more hope for a fool than for him. (Proverbs 26:12)

Second, the church doesn't need a spiritual criminal – a person who has no intention of being saved from his or her sins. Their true colors will show eventually. In spite of their profession of faith, they still lie and steal and destroy and hurt. All the preaching in the world, and all the discipline in the world, make no impression on them. They are there to satisfy themselves, and everyone around them is a potential victim. And the church is a good hunting ground for them because Christians are supposed to respond to such behavior with forbearance and forgiveness!

> For certain men whose condemnation was written about long ago have secretly slipped in among you. They are godless men, who change the grace of our God into a license for immorality and deny Jesus Christ our only Sovereign and Lord. (Jude 4)

Neither of these kinds of people will respond favorably to discipline. You may as well save your breath. Eventually, if you keep the pressure of discipline pounding at their door, they'll leave the church and everyone will be relieved and get back to the business at hand.

> When the wicked rise to power, people go into hiding; but when the wicked perish, the righteous thrive. (Proverbs 28:28)

What the church *does* need is the kind of person Jesus describes in the Sermon on the Mount.

> Blessed are the poor in spirit, for theirs is the kingdom of Heaven.
>
> Blessed are those who mourn, for they will be comforted.
>
> Blessed are the meek, for they will inherit the earth.
>
> Blessed are those who hunger and thirst for righteousness, for they will be filled.
>
> Blessed are the merciful, for they will be shown mercy.
>
> Blessed are the pure in heart, for they will see God.
>
> Blessed are the peacemakers, for they will be called sons of God.
>
> Blessed are those who are persecuted because of righteousness, for theirs is the kingdom of Heaven.
>
> Blessed are you when people insult you, persecute you and falsely say all kinds of evil against you because of me.
>
> Rejoice and be glad, because great is your reward in Heaven, for in the same way they persecuted the prophets who were before you. (Matthew 5:3-12)

This kind of person responds willingly to discipline, of any form. You don't have to tell them twice! They *want* to learn

The Disciplined Christian Life

more – they show up to learn as much as possible of the things of God and about salvation. They *want* to examine their hearts for any sin there. They *want* to change their behavior; they willingly admit to having failed both God and man in the past. They *want* to submit to those in authority over them, because they realize that these shepherds have been given the responsibility to lead them to God and life. They *want* peace – in their own hearts first, and between themselves and God and between themselves and others.

People like this are a joy to work with. Would to God that every church, and every professing Christian, were this willing to submit to discipline. Then the passage in Hebrews would come true.

> How much more should we submit to the Father of our spirits and live! (Hebrews 12:9)

It takes the right attitude, it takes obedience, it takes hard work, and it takes the Spirit of Christ making us willing to walk in his way of life. As Jesus submitted to his Father, we also submit joyfully to correction and discipline.

> Let us fix our eyes on Jesus, the author and perfecter of our faith, who for the joy set before him endured the cross, scorning its shame, and sat down at the right hand of the throne of God. (Hebrews 12:2)

The leaders of the church (the good ones, at any rate! – not every church or church leader is on board with God's program) are trained and willing to help you in your journey to Heaven. Their job, if they're doing it right, will be twofold: to help you get free of your sin, and to get you ready to live with God in his spiritual world. This is the Mission of the church, and this is *all* that they are able to help you do as church leaders. More than this they aren't called to do, and probably aren't able to do.

> Silver or gold I do not have, but what I have I give you. In the name of Jesus Christ of Nazareth, walk. (Acts 3:6)

But they are the only people on the planet who can do this most important of all jobs! Christ has given them the spiritual gifts necessary to carry out this Mission. So when you come to a church, you make their job much easier if you willingly submit to their ministry in these two areas. Otherwise there's no point in your going.

> Obey your leaders and submit to their authority. They keep watch over you as men who must give an account. Obey them so that their work will be a joy, not a burden, for that would be of no advantage to you. (Hebrews 13:17)

What will discipline look like?

For the answer to this question, let's go back to Paul's counsel to Timothy.

> All Scripture is God-breathed and is useful for teaching, rebuking, correcting and training in righteousness, so that the man of God may be thoroughly equipped for every good work. (2 Timothy 3:16-17)

Notice that he starts with Scripture. This is the foundation of all discipline – otherwise what will happen in a church is only the work of man; churches become little kingdoms where men appropriate the glory and authority due to Christ alone and force the members to do their bidding. It's true that men must carry out the work of discipline in the church, but we know that it will be *Christ's* kingdom when they carefully follow the instructions in Christ's Word. God will honor his Word, and he will give success to those who build his Kingdom using his materials. "For no one can lay any foundation other than the one already laid, which is Jesus Christ." (1 Corinthians 3:11)

That Word will empower and guide the church to do the following types of activities.

- ***Teaching*** – This takes many forms in the church. The obvious ones are the preaching and teaching that the church leaders do every Sunday. But there are other settings where teaching is going on – for example, the older women are told to instruct the younger women, parents are told to instruct their children, and elders are to lead young men by example.

  The importance of teaching is based on the fact that we are learning creatures. Our heads are the first target of truth – through our eyes and ears, we take in information and process it in our brains. Our minds have to grasp the truth first, since the mind is the seat of all that we do and say.

  > Do not conform any longer to the pattern of this world, but be transformed by the renewing of your mind. Then you will be able to test and approve what God's will is – his good, pleasing and perfect will. (Romans 12:2)

  From there the mind affects the heart with its emotions and feelings. In other words, truth guides our hearts – not the other way around.

  How much teaching should go on in the church? Well, like a child growing up, we need to learn the basics first – what Hebrews 5:12 refers to. Then as we get older we learn more of what the world is like and how to make our way around in it. I guess it depends on what your aspirations are – if you're content to live on the bottom rung, with only a low-level job and barely getting along, twelve years of school should suffice. But if you want to honor God with your entire life and do your utmost for him, it will take a lifetime to learn all about God and his Kingdom. There is no such thing as learning too much about this amazing new world that God has for his people.

- **Rebuking** – Oh that the modern church knew more of this blessing! "An honest answer is like a kiss on the lips." (Proverbs 24:26) People have an entirely wrong view of a rebuke. When given in love – and our brothers, including the elders, do it out of love for us – it is designed to help us. Instead, people get insulted and either lash back in anger or leave the church. What a pity.

This is no time for pride. The Mission of the church is to save us from our sin. If we don't believe that then perhaps we ought to save everyone else a lot of trouble and stay home! We are sinners; we are not perfect people, and we are not yet ready to live with God – not the way we are now. There is a lot of cleanup to be done in our hearts and lives. A true Christian who wants to be saved from sin will not back away from this truth but rather eagerly look for opportunities to address the problem.

It *is* the church's business to address your sin. People suffering from adult pride don't want anybody else meddling in their private lives. Though it's true that the elders shouldn't follow you home and put everything you do to a test – it's your business to clean your own face, spiritually, since you know best where you are dirty – it isn't true that you are thereby safe from having to face your sins in church. The sermons are going to address your sin, your brothers will be offended by it, and you must reach out and eagerly take the medicine for your soul offered to you in the ministry of the church if you hope to gain eternal life.

It's a spiritually healthy exercise to act like the tax collector when you're at church. He came humbly, ready to be talked to, admitting he was not pure but in great need of salvation. As Jesus said, *this* kind of person goes home from church accepted by God. He went there for the right thing, and he got it. (Luke 18:13-14)

And how many church crises could we avoid if people were more open to being rebuked! We punish children when they don't listen to a rebuke to stop unacceptable behavior; we know that, if they'll simply listen and do what we say, the situation will get straightened out and we can go back to business. We don't hate them! It therefore frustrates us when they don't respond positively and change; getting mad at us only makes matters worse.

But in the church, pride gets in the way and makes it impossible to work things out. *It's the mark of a true Christian to accept a rebuke when deserved –* and God makes it plain in his Word when we deserve it. If you turn away from that rebuke and leave, you lose. You may never get another chance at salvation if you despise God's Word and authority over you like that. It's the very definition of sin itself to reject the rebuke out of pride. So tread carefully.

> He who listens to a life-giving rebuke will be at home among the wise. (Proverbs 15:31)

- ***Correcting*** – This is the testing part of discipline and almost never done in today's churches. In schools the teachers will give the students a test to see how much they've learned in a subject. The test isn't designed to depress the students about what they couldn't remember. It's designed to point out to them the areas they still need help in. It's an examination of what they know compared to what they ought to know, what they really need to know, if they want to master the subject. It's that examination aspect that we don't do in church.

Let's use an example to illustrate this necessary feature of discipline. I've heard a lot of prayers from church members over the years. All kinds of prayers. Usually people pray whatever pops into their heads and hearts on the spur of the moment. It is, as one writer lamented once, the least practiced and least prepared-for part of worship.

But for all the fervency of these prayers, they rarely measured up to Biblical standards. The Bible tells us plainly how to approach God in prayer. It tells us what the agenda of prayer should be. It tells us when to pray. It shows us model prayers from experienced prayer warriors. And yet, even though the Bible is so specific about what prayer should be like, I've seen almost no attempt to apply those standards to the way people pray today in church. It's as if they don't want to be bothered with God's instructions on prayer! They often won't even bring a Bible to the prayer service!

People aren't testing what they are doing against the Word of God. I guess that pastors are so thankful when a person wants to do *anything* in the church that they are really reluctant to put their actions to the test. But letting anything happen is fatal to the life of the church. Not just any sacrifice offered will do – we learn that from the Old Testament. Good intentions aren't enough – we have to live by the truth of God.

Aaron's sons were killed because they offered a sacrifice of their own design to God. Uzzah was struck dead because he violated the principles of how to approach God's holy altar. Saul was dethroned because he changed God's commands just a little bit to something more reasonable to him. God refused to listen to Israel's prayers because they still harbored sin in their hearts. The point is that we can't make up what we will do to please God; we have to do things in the way he specified – and that requires correcting our actions to fit his standards.

There is a true faith and a false faith; there are good works that please God and "good" works that don't please him; there is prayer that reaches his throne and prayer that doesn't; there is acceptable warfare against the enemy and unacceptable warfare; there are God's ways and man's ways. Now unless you're as wise as Jesus is, you're going to get a lot of this wrong before you get it right. Your willingness to be corrected will make the difference between success and failure.

> Examine yourselves to see whether you are in the faith; test yourselves. Do you not realize that Christ Jesus is in you – unless, of course, you fail the test? (2 Corinthians 13:5)

- ***Training in righteousness*** – This too is almost never done in the church. Training is a long procedure of drills to get the material or exercise firmly embedded in the mind and instinct. The military, again, provides a useful model. The drill sergeant puts his poor recruits through endless drills day after day. After weeks and months of constant drills and training the soldiers are thoroughly sick of training! The beauty of this training program is this – when they are actually in combat, in the middle of a situation that they trained for, the necessary actions are instinctive. They move quickly, efficiently, and effectively. They succeed. And it was all because of the thoroughness of the training.

The typical church almost never trains its people for anything. Sunday after Sunday they sit passively and listen to a sermon they often can't follow and almost never remember. They go to fellowship meals. They help out in fund drives. In fact, church has turned into having the most fun and expending the least effort – by design. Not only are they not training in spiritual matters, they don't even know why they are there!

The Mission of the church is to get us all out of our sins and living a righteous life. But though we are often *told* to do that, there is no training for it. Probably even church leaders wouldn't know where to start on this. How does one *train for righteousness*?

Let's start at the beginning. Hebrews gives us the first step in the way of righteousness.

> Anyone who lives on milk, being still an infant, is not acquainted with the teaching about righteousness. But solid food is for the mature, who by constant use have trained themselves to distinguish good from evil. (Hebrews 5:13-14)

First you have to learn what righteousness is. We don't have to go to man's systems of morality to find out – in fact, we must not. God's Word alone specifies what righteousness is. This will take a lot of studying the Bible – both Old and New Testaments.

Next, you have to understand that only Jesus is righteous according to the definition of righteousness – the Law of God. The corollary of that truth is that we are not righteous; we will never in ourselves measure up to God's standards.

The solution is to wear, take upon ourselves, be covered with, the righteousness of Christ – that is, if we have any hope of living with God in Heaven. Nobody will be allowed in without this perfect righteousness of the Son of God.

How does one take on this righteousness? Only through faith – and our forefather Abraham "discovered" how to do this in his day. (Romans 4:1)

The Disciplined Christian Life

Faith is one of the spiritual abilities that the Holy Spirit gives us upon conversion. In fact, as we follow the Spirit – we dare not follow the Law itself! – we will learn how to live in this perfect righteousness of Christ. (See Paul's argument in Galatians 1-3.)

Next, you will need the spirit of Joseph to start turning away from the sins and temptations that used to appeal to you. This is going to be very difficult and will take some time to get good at. Just when you think you've mastered a certain temptation, it comes roaring back with unexpected force. Why in the world did I do that again? So we are weaker than we think, and we don't yet understand how to stand in the power and purity of Christ as we ought.

> So I find this law at work: When I want to do good, evil is right there with me. For in my inner being I delight in God's Law; but I see another law at work in the members of my body, waging war against the law of my mind and making me a prisoner of the law of sin at work within my members. What a wretched man I am! Who will rescue me from this body of death? (Romans 7:21-24)

> For the grace of God that brings salvation has appeared to all men. It teaches us to say "No" to ungodliness and worldly passions, and to live self-controlled, upright and godly lives in this present age. (Titus 2:11-12)

> Those who belong to Christ Jesus have crucified the sinful nature with its passions and desires. Since we live by the Spirit, let us keep in step with the Spirit. (Galatians 5:24-25)

The point is that that this requires a dedicated heart, a learning mind, the power of God, lots of opportunities, humility in the face of failure and thankfulness to God in success, and *time*. Training like this doesn't come easily or quickly.

Discipline happens best in the church. In fact, it's only real chance of success is in the setting of the church. The resources and spiritual gifts are there, the personnel and experts in spiritual care are there, the opportunities are there. So who in their right minds would pass up this opportunity to be saved to the uttermost?

Almost everyone, it seems! People aren't willing to admit their spiritual needs to others, and they prefer to work on whatever shortcomings they think they may have on their own, at home, where nobody else will know about it. This is both foolish and futile. It will almost never happen. So many have tried this way and failed. It's far better to just go to the hospital and get the surgery done instead of attempting it on your own at home in your kitchen.

Besides, God *commanded* you to submit to the discipline of the church. He designed the church for your salvation; he knows what he's doing.

What is life without discipline?

When a body doesn't get exercise, it gets flabby and out of shape. It can't keep up with the demands of daily life like it used to. It can't fight off sickness either. Health experts tell us that even a regular program of walking will do wonders for our stamina and good health. But even armed with that information, few people take the time and trouble to do themselves some good.

The Disciplined Christian Life

So it's no wonder that the same undisciplined, lazy, devil-may-care attitude exists in the church. People are naturally lazy, and they generally won't do anything till you make them do it. The problem is that the consequences of the lack of spiritual discipline are truly catastrophic – they affect our eternal future.

You have no doubt met the student who rebelled in class and declared that "I'm not doing this! I'll never need this!" We who are mature pity such a student. Unless he sees his mistake, the chances are really good that he'll end up a criminal or a social deadweight or parasite. At best he'll only be able to land a bottom-level job and struggle daily with failure and frustration. It's hard for some people to think *long-term* – they don't see that training now means benefits later.

Unfortunately the same thing happens in the church. There will be many who refuse to submit to spiritual discipline. **Mark them.** They will, in due time, become the spiritual criminals and deadbeats that drag our churches down. They will be the ones saying ignorant things in church meetings, clogging up the works with the ways of the world instead of God's will, volunteering for jobs that they aren't qualified to do. To get anything real done in the church, the leaders will have to deal with these people sharply and either get them out of the way or change them. They are going to be a blight on the life of the church.

It's easy to tell if there is a good system of discipline in a church – if you're using the right measuring stick. For example, most churches rely on the members to take care of themselves, usually at home after the service, and they have no way of measuring whether people really are changing as a result of the ministry. This is not good. This is a lack of discipline on the church level. The leadership can't have such a casual attitude about whether their work is bearing fruit. It's true that we can't make fruit happen – only God does that. But pastors and teachers have to have their finger on the pulse of their flock in order to bring the Word to bear on the needs of the people. They have to lead the people *somewhere*. If nobody is studying, or praying, or living a holy life, then something is wrong and this problem must be addressed.

At the very least, people living in sin must be faced with the demands of God in the Word and shown the way of escape. At the very least, the ministry should be holding out the hope of Heaven and preparing people for that final transition from this world. If churches aren't working on these two issues, what in the world do they think they are here to do?

These are bad signs in any church, a sure indicator that the church that operates like this doesn't understand the importance of church discipline.

- *There's no accountability* – everyone is doing what they want to do, nobody is doing what God told them to do, and the leaders are taking no forthright action to straighten problems out. Everyone has an opinion, everyone has a vote, and anything could happen. In fact, some very unacceptable things *do* happen in a situation like this and nobody can do anything about it. People feel free to leave over some slight pretext – wounded pride, failed power plays, getting caught in sin, petty squabbles. There is no way to hold people's feet to the fire, because there are no standards and nobody is authorized to implement them if there were.
- *Nobody is changing* – sinners remain sinners and nobody sees the problem in that. Everyone is comfortable in what little they know and the little that they agree to do for the church and God. As long as they don't see each other for more than an hour on Sunday morning, they get along fine. But when a

crisis comes up, you can tell that all the sermons and lessons had no effect on their sinful natures – the poison is still in their hearts and comes pouring out. They manifest the works of the flesh instead of the fruit of the Spirit. They will even feel justified in acting like this toward one another!

- *No real work is being done* – people are going through the motions of church, but the real work of the Kingdom of God goes begging. Committees, picnics, sports events, bake sales, youth outings, fund raisers – lots of busy work but nothing that pertains to the Mission. Even the sermons and lessons steer away from the King's business and focus on anything but – like current events, the enemy down the road, and what wonderful Christians we all are, and how much fun we are having.

- *Leaders resort to tricks to keep the church going* – as if the church consists of consumers that the leaders have to entertain and keep happy or they'll leave. We have to have trinkets and prizes for the kids. We have to change the music to suit the taste of the unbelievers or they won't come to church. We have to keep the sermons short, the music long, the demands on their time minimal, the number of meetings low, drop-down screens with pictures to keep their attention during the sermon, videos to entertain them. After all, the theory goes, we are in competition with modern times and we have to provide *more* stimulation for their senses than the world will or we won't keep their interest!

I've got news for you – if your church is like this, you've lost already. You may as well close the doors because you're not going to accomplish the Mission that the Lord has given you. Not only have you lost the sense of the Mission, but you'll never keep the troops together to "fight the good fight of faith." The complete lack of *discipline* will be your spiritual downfall.

A lack of discipline on the church level will lead to disastrous effects in people's private lives. Unless the church is rigorously following the Lord's guidelines in how to "equip the saints," the unthinkable will happen – they will continue to wallow around in their sins and ignorance. The Problem, remember, of mankind is *sin* – rebellion against God and his Kingdom. Discipline addresses that Problem. Therefore, no discipline – no salvation – a life of sin. It's that simple and fatal.

> Timothy, my son, I give you this instruction in keeping with the prophecies once made about you, so that by following them you may fight the good fight, holding on to faith and a good conscience. Some have rejected these and so have shipwrecked their faith. (1 Timothy 1:18-19)

> If they have escaped the corruption of the world by knowing our Lord and Savior Jesus Christ and are again entangled in it and overcome, they are worse off at the end than they were at the beginning. It would have been better for them not to have known the way of righteousness, than to have known it and then to turn their backs on the sacred command that was passed on to them. Of them the proverbs are true: "A dog returns to its vomit," and, "A sow that is washed goes back to her wallowing in the mud." (2 Peter 2:20-22)

The Christian life

A disciplined Christian life requires a person who loves God, hates sin, and loves righteousness.

- God demands nothing less than perfection from us; he deserves nothing less. So the disciplined Christian is determined, out of love for the God who loves him and saved him, to give God his best.

- Sin is an ugly thing in God's creation, and the least trace of sin is unbecoming to the child of God. So the disciplined Christian will study how to eradicate all traces of sin from his heart and mind, and take advantage of all God's spiritual resources to accomplish this task. He will also learn how to protect himself from all influences that would take him back to sin.

- Righteousness is a beautiful thing to behold – perfect obedience, perfect submission to the will of God, perfect love, perfect joy in God. The disciplined Christian, knowing that only in Christ will he be so perfect, will not rest until he is "clothed with Christ." Then the Father will be pleased with him.

Know then in your heart that as a man disciplines his son, so the LORD your God disciplines you. Observe the commands of the LORD your God, walking in his ways and revering him. For the LORD your God is bringing you into a good land. (Deuteronomy 8:5-7)

A Church for Christians

A Church for Christians

Christ's church is designed for Christians. It meets their specific needs. As they grow in their new life before God, they will find the resources and functions for spiritual growth in the church. By God's design, the two fit together – and it's a perfect fit.

At least that's the idea.

Perhaps many of our churches started out with this in mind, but over the years (centuries?) there have been many changes to the agenda. What passes for "church" now is often just a rehash of the world's entertainment industry. The original focus has been lost; new Christians aren't finding what they need in these churches. It's no wonder that there's been a mass exodus out of today's churches as disillusioned sheep look elsewhere for what they need.

If you are starting a new church, you would do well to take stock first and find out precisely what Christians need from God's house. If you lay the right foundation now, the church will stand for a long time in strength and usefulness to God's people. If you don't know what believers are going to need, however, you will probably lay the foundation on "sand" – see Jesus' warning in Matthew 7 – and the church will fall; it's just a matter of time.

If you are already in a church and things aren't going well, you have two options: either change the foundations (and doing that is like performing heart surgery! It can be done, but it won't be at all easy), or leave and go find a healthy church. The point is that you can't continue under a ministry that doesn't help you.

The church has such an important role to play in this fallen world that we have to take great care when we form a church. We can't just do as we please and call it Christ's church. Either we achieve the Mission that Christ has assigned to us, or we're wasting our time and his.

There are deadly problems in this world, and the church is the only organization that can deal with those problems. God has given us special resources that worldly organizations don't have. We aren't called to do things the way the world does; those ways can't save a person from his sin, nor its consequences. When a person runs into problems that this world can't help him with, the church becomes a haven to him. Here he will find spiritual help for the troubles of his soul, firepower from Heaven against his enemies, a new family that is dedicated to help him make his way from this world to the next one. While the world focuses on the temporal, the church turns its attention to the spiritual and eternal – and it satisfies the deepest needs of the human spirit.

Why are we at church?

Unfortunately, too many churches have come together haphazardly with no specific goal in mind. They didn't really research this business of God's church. They either satisfied themselves with a few popular Scripture passages about church life, or they simply made up their own agenda. They didn't get at the depth of what a church has to be – you can tell that they didn't, because they still run their churches in a superficial way. Confusion reigns: very few of the members really know what they are doing there.

People come to church for all sorts of reasons. Most of those reasons, unfortunately, are things that they made up themselves – to satisfy their conscience, to do God a favor, to present a favorable community image, for fellowship, family counseling, mate-seeking, for tradition's sake, enjoyment of a worship service, entertainment, to voice their opinions, or for political reasons. But if this is all that you are looking for, there are a lot of other organizations that will also fit the bill. What makes the church unique among them all?

The church is unique by virtue of its Mission. If other organizations that man puts together were capable of solving our spiritual problems, Jesus wouldn't have bothered to set up the church. The reason he came to earth, however, was to bring real solutions to the problems that none of us were able to solve. He put special powers and knowledge into this new organization – his church – so that "whosoever will" may come here and find relief for their spirits. The church has something that no other organization has, or ever will have.

Our calling

To understand the Mission, we first have to understand our calling. *We are called to live with God.* [1] We see this in many places in the Bible, both Old and New Testaments. For example, here's a picture of that goal in the book of Revelation.

> Then I saw a new Heaven and a new earth, for the first heaven and the first earth had passed away, and there was no longer any sea. I saw the Holy City, the new Jerusalem, coming down out of Heaven from God, prepared as a bride beautifully dressed for her husband. And I heard a loud voice from the throne saying, "Now the dwelling of God is with men, and he will live with them. They will be his people, and God himself will be with them and be their God. He will wipe every tear from their eyes. There will be no more

---

[1] One of the Confessions of Faith states it like this: "Man's chief end is to glorify God, and to enjoy him forever."

death or mourning or crying or pain, for the old order of things has passed away." (Revelation 21:1-4)

Someday we are going to leave this world and go live with God. We are "living stones" of the new Temple in which God will live. Jesus has gone to Heaven to prepare this new home for us. We will live and reign with Christ, at God's right hand. The idea is astounding, that a former rebel, liar and murderer would be pardoned and – not only restored, but – lifted up to be one of God's own family.

The conversion experience brings sinner and God together for the first time. Suddenly this person is aware of the holiness of God, the majesty of God, the wisdom of God, the power of God, the beauty of God. He sees now that God is the fulfillment of all his desires and needs. Heaven no longer is a far-away, strange, unknown place. ***Heaven is where God is*** – and that's why he wants to go there, to be with this God.

There are two problems in the way, however. The **first** one is that *no sinner is allowed into Heaven.* This is a serious issue with God. We may not think that sin is such a big deal; but to God, sin is insolence, treason, and highly destructive. Look at what a single sin of rebellion did at the beginning of the world! Adam and Eve's sin plunged the entire world into death and destruction. That's not going to happen again in Heaven, in God's new creation. "Since we have these promises, dear friends, let us purify ourselves from everything that contaminates body and spirit, perfecting holiness out of reverence for God." (2 Corinthians 7:1) But we are steeped in sin, and sin is ingrained like a stain in our thoughts and attitudes. If it were up to us, we could never clean this stain of sin from our lives to the extent that God would be satisfied with us. The perfection of Heaven is a standard that is completely beyond our ability to achieve.

The **second** problem is that *Heaven is spiritual, and we are still very physical.* We are governed by our five senses: we know and love what we can see and feel, and we have almost no comprehension of a God that we can't see. We don't appreciate spiritual treasures because we don't see what benefit they give us in this material world. We have made secure little nests for ourselves in this physical world, but we would be totally lost in the halls of Heaven – a strange place to us. It's a mystery to me why people think they want to go to Heaven when they know nothing about it! Perhaps they think that Heaven is like the nirvana that the pagan religions teach about: just an extension of this world's pleasures. It's not. It's a spiritual place, not a physical world. As Paul says, we must *change* in order to go to Heaven – "I declare to you, brothers, that flesh and blood cannot inherit the kingdom of God, nor does the perishable inherit the imperishable." (1 Corinthians 15:50) So the only way we can be made ready for Heaven is to die to this world, and be raised as spiritual. And that, too, is beyond our ability to achieve.

The Mission

So, Jesus set up the church to work on these two problems. The Mission of the church is twofold:

- **First**, we have to be thoroughly delivered of our sins – our immorality, our waywardness, our ignorance, our willfulness, our rebellion, our lawlessness, our independent attitude. The job of the Christian is to come back to God, humble himself, submit to God's rule, and serve him. We have to *change*, from sinner to saint. The ministry of the church *has* to address that need, if we have any hope of living with a holy and righteous God.

- **Second**, we have to start getting used to the new world that Jesus is preparing for us. We have to put our minds on things above, learn about God and his ways, live in the righteousness of Christ, start frequenting the Temple in Heaven, wean ourselves away from this physical world and start storing up treasures in Heaven, learn to be holy and set apart for God's use. Heaven is not for strangers, but for God's family who feel at home there.

There's a lot to be done in these two areas. It's surprising that so many people are doing hardly anything to address these key issues and yet they still have hopes of Heaven someday. It will take all the resources of a church's ministry to successfully prepare its members for this kind of life. I know, it's not much fun to focus on your sin when you go to church. It's like finding out that we have cancer, or going through a heart attack. It's not exactly what we were planning to do with our free time! But this problem has been forced upon us, and now we have to deal with it or die. *The Bible's entire message revolves around this issue of what is going to be done about our sin* – otherwise we have no hope of living with God.

People naturally want the church to address other problems in their lives – family problems, job problems, neighbor problems, financial problems, health problems. But Christians have to understand that these, though important, are *not* the primary Mission of the church. These other issues will be addressed, even some of them solved, *only if people focus on the two main issues of our faith*. If we make real progress on the primary Mission, that will start straightening out other problems along the way.

There's another aspect of this truth. If you're in a church that you're having doubts about – if you're wondering if you should stay there – put the church to this test. Look for these two aspects of the Mission. If they are there, then the church really is helping you; you may have problems with it, but they aren't fatal. That church is helping you achieve your goal; the problems that come up along the way are only secondary issues, and you would do better to stay and work them out than leave a vital church and go starving somewhere else.

But if that church isn't helping you at all to achieve spiritual growth, then it's time to go. You are not obligated to sit down to a table that has no food – that's ridiculous. You have to recognize that not every church understands the Mission. Though no church is perfect, there are some that understand what you need to achieve your goal of Heaven. Find them and learn from them.

Plan for success

People love to organize their churches around special programs and activities and functions that satisfy certain "needs" of theirs. Many churches are like this. But the only church that can claim Christ's blessing is the one which is helping its members achieve their spiritual calling – to someday be ready and fit to live with God. All those other side-shows can, and often do, cloud the real issue. **The church is a special agency to help Christians achieve their goal of Heaven.** You will be able to tell, when you go into a church, whether they are doing God's work there – or whether they are catering to man's physical desires instead. If people are changing from sinners to saints, and if their minds and hearts are on the treasures of Heaven, then that church is doing Christ's work. Otherwise you may as well go outside and look for the name "Ichabod" over the front door.

As you've probably guessed by now, putting together a church that is focused and on-task doesn't happen by accident. You have to specifically structure the church in such a way that the Mission is easily carried out there, and "extracurricular" activities that take away from the Mission will be hard to include in the program. There have to be certain things in place for a church to run this race without interference from man's worldly and sinful opinions getting in the way. It may seem heartless to be so focused, so "hard-line" about working on the Mission like this. But it's for everyone's good. If you let yourself stray from the Mission, people will definitely have more "fun" in church but they won't be ready for Judgment Day. And then what will you say to the Lord of the church who assigned you a task to do, and you spent your energies making church more fun for people and catering to their whims instead of saving their souls?

It's time to think through this issue about the church. Why are we here? What are we here to accomplish? Are we reaching these goals of ours? If not, where do we need to change? What's getting in the way of us reaching our goals? Are we self-satisfied and hard-hearted like the Israelites in the Promised Land, no longer able to hear the voice of the Lord? Or are we "lean and mean," "beating our bodies" for self-discipline, and able to run the race? Is our church no different than the world's entertainment centers, or is it a well-disciplined army fighting its way through this world to achieve the next world?

A new business will make a business plan, because making profits doesn't happen by accident. It takes a lot of forethought and resources to make it happen. The military spends a huge amount of its time planning and accumulating resources before going out into the field of battle. A church, too, should plan and organize for success. People don't get saved, or get ready for Heaven, by accident. True, you may find people in a lazy church who are nevertheless getting ready for Heaven – but that's probably because someone else is working on them, not the church they are in. Their own church is failing them, while some other ministry has to take up the slack.

What we want to look at now are some foundation stones for a successful church. This is not to say that these are the only things that must be in a church; but when planning a church, one first looks at the most important issues. Other ingredients for a church can and will be added to the picture as time goes on. But we are saying that if you don't have these essentials, your church won't work – the Christians (if there are any!) in your assembly will not find what they need to achieve their spiritual goals. For example, you can be missing an evangelistic team for a while and still be a church, though you'll probably be wanting to add that down the road for future growth. But your church can't survive – it will never grow – if you don't understand who the Head of the church is. The body may be missing a hand and still survive; but it can't live without the Head.

Most churches will be careful to put together a program with the "essentials" – or what they think are the essentials. But this requires more than a superficial planning session. The preacher, the Sunday School teachers, facilities, a structured worship service, and so on will get a "church" off to a start that may be encouraging and, at first, successful. But over time, you may begin to realize that your planning session overlooked a few fundamental realities that could have given your church more strength, vitality, and permanence. Your church may be experiencing problems it can't solve, or it's foundering over sticky issues for some unknown reason. With a little foresight, you could have built a few additional elements into the foundation that would have made the difference in the long run.

True Christians are coming into your church for help. Are you going to be ready for them? Can you give them what they need to get ready for Heaven? Are you going to stick to your program and give them what they *need*, not what they want? Are you clear about the Mission, and focused on it? Remember that, though they might be Christians, you are going to have to lead them to eternal life, and that will require discipline on your part – they may not have that discipline yet. Only the church that firmly but gently prepares its members for Heaven will receive Christ's commendation on Judgment Day.

The other side of this coin is what the individual Christian sees in your church. If he is there for the right reason, he *needs* a church that understands the Mission and how to accomplish it. He doesn't want a church that will waste his time with trivia. "My sheep know my voice." The true Christian will recognize the work of his Master in the local church and willingly fit into the program. But he can also recognize a cheat. He knows when the church is led by "hirelings" who aren't in step with Christ's agenda. He would be justified in leaving such a church and finding one that is built on the right foundation.

> For no one can lay any foundation other than the one already laid, which is Jesus Christ. (1 Corinthians 3:11)

The Church – the Kingdom of God

Our Father in Heaven, hallowed be your Name, your kingdom come, your will be done on earth as it is in Heaven. (Matthew 6:9)

The first order of business when putting together a church is to *organize* it. And most churches organize in some fashion – in fact, this is one important aspect that makes denominations different from one another; they organize along different lines. However, it's not our purpose to judge between denominations or churches about their forms of government. What we want to look at is whether they understand the foundation of a true church government – that Christ is the King.

There can be only one King in a kingdom. And if the word "kingdom" means anything at all, the church isn't a democracy. Christ alone rules over his people, and we are all his servants. But this is such a foreign concept to many modern Christians that it rarely forms a real part of the local church. We usually do anything but follow the rule of Christ! So it's no wonder that many of our churches are failing in the Mission. They can't possibly succeed until they get a good hold of this idea of Christ's kingdom.

Christ is Lord

When we first became Christians, we were immediately faced with the reality of the preeminence of Christ over us. At least that was the formula that we learned; evidently it takes some people a lot of time to learn just what those words mean.

> If you confess with your mouth, "Jesus is Lord," and believe in your heart that God raised him from the dead, you will be saved. (Romans 10:9)

The new convert is at first anxious to do Christ's will. He willingly submits to whatever Jesus would have for him to do. But over time, our "flesh nature" starts creeping back in and we return to the way we used to live – doing whatever we want to do. It requires too much effort to study the will of Christ (the Bible), and it requires crucifying our flesh to make room for the working of the Spirit in our hearts – a painful and tedious process.

Perhaps nobody explained to us, at the beginning, why it's so important that Jesus is the King of the church.

- *First,* this is his creation. The Bible says that God created the world through Christ – a fundamental aspect of this universe that will have far-reaching consequences for everyone in the end. He who creates, owns; and he who owns, controls. In order to fix this creation of God's that we have broken, Jesus is given the *right* and the *power* to rule over it and steer it back into his purposes.

- *Second,* the original problem of mankind is sin – which is rebellion against the King. "Sin is lawlessness," the Bible tells us. (1 John 3:4) That rebellion has to be eliminated; your independent attitude has to change completely. You will be surprised how many times this issue will come up between you and the King. Your lawlessness is deeper than you can imagine. And his determination to rule over you is for your good; he intends to completely cure you and bless you with the treasures of Heaven.

So, in light of the need, Jesus brings us into a special relationship to him that will directly address that need. Our duty is to submit to this King so that we might be saved from our sin and take our place in his Kingdom. ***The task of the King is to make you a willing subject in his Kingdom*** – and that will require the work of a lifetime!

What will the King do?

We Americans take our freedom seriously; we always have. We will fight for the right to rule ourselves. We little appreciate what it means to live in a kingdom. So it's no wonder that we don't understand, and we don't like, the idea of being ruled over even in the church – we would rather rule over ourselves.

We may have good reasons for wanting our country's political system to run this way, but such an attitude is deadly in the church. *The church is not a democracy – it's a kingdom.* Jesus never gave us a choice in this matter; he simply took charge and insists on ruling us. If we don't understand or appreciate the importance of Jesus' rule over us, then we will never be saved from what is killing us.

First let's review the situation. We are sinners – rebels against God's rule, independent and willing to fight for our freedom from all rule. We are unable to change this attitude in us; try though we might, we are unable nor do we want to follow God's Law of righteousness. It came from eating that fruit in the Garden of Eden.

As a result, our society is filled with abominations and destruction.

> They have become filled with every kind of wickedness, evil, greed and depravity. They are full of

> envy, murder, strife, deceit and malice. They are gossips, slanderers, God-haters, insolent, arrogant and boastful; they invent ways of doing evil; they disobey their parents; they are senseless, faithless, heartless, ruthless. Although they know God's righteous decree that those who do such things deserve death, they not only continue to do these very things but also approve of those who practice them. (Romans 1:29-32)

The people who had the best chance at actually becoming a righteous people, who would measure up to God's standard of perfection, were the Jews – and they failed miserably.

> For I could wish that I myself were cursed and cut off from Christ for the sake of my brothers, those of my own race, the people of Israel. Theirs is the adoption as sons; theirs the divine glory, the covenants, the receiving of the Law, the temple worship and the promises. Theirs are the Patriarchs, and from them is traced the human ancestry of Christ, who is God over all, forever praised! Amen. It is not as though God's Word had failed. For not all who are descended from Israel are Israel. (Romans 9:3-6)

> As it is written: "God's name is blasphemed among the Gentiles because of you." (Romans 2:24)

If it were possible for us to achieve righteousness on our own, Christ would not have had to come. But since we were helpless and without hope, Jesus came to do for us what we couldn't do – lift us out of sin and death, and set us in Heaven. Now we are free, as Paul tells us, to live for God.

It's not as if a new Christian is self-sufficient, however. He has now become one with Christ for a very good reason: from now on, *Jesus will live in and through him.* This believer is now on his way to Heaven, powered by Christ's Spirit. But if he would lose Christ's Spirit, his continuous presence, his supplies and strength, his hope also would be gone. Jesus must rule and lead and carry this person step by step, all the way to his goal. That's why Jesus promised him, "Never will I leave you; never will I forsake you." (Hebrews 13:5) To do that would be to remove his very life and breath from the believer.

So the job of the King is ongoing, and it covers every aspect of their journey to Heaven.

- ***The King sets the standards and publishes his will.*** The Bible is key to the ministry of the church. It's really unfortunate that, in our day and age, almost nobody takes the Bible seriously anymore. The Liberals, and the cults, have stripped the Bible of its authority and credibility, to the point that a person who actually believes it and tries to live by it appears naïve in our society. But to the King, the Bible is his will for his people.

  The Bible lays out the entire program for God's people. It describes God, the goal of their journey. It shows them the new world of God that they are headed for. It lays down the ground rules for living in God's Kingdom. It reveals the resources that are available to them. It shows the way out of this world, and the road to Heaven. It lays out the overall war-plan for God's people as they struggle against a resisting Enemy. Without this full description at their disposal, the people of God would be entirely in the dark and quite unable to reach their goal. It's a spiritual book; nothing like it has ever appeared in this world. Christians know that they have to put their own opinions and prejudices aside when they read it, because in spite of the fact that it doesn't make sense to the average (darkened!) rational mind, it really does shine the light on the situation before them like nothing else will.

The truth of the Bible is not negotiable. These are the King's orders. These are the King's principles. If you don't like what the Bible says, you will find yourself on the outside of his house. Probably your dislike toward the Bible actually comes from a dislike for God, because the Bible's purpose is simply to reveal God and his world to us. For those who are destined for life with the God of the Bible, however, his Word is precious to them and indispensable.

- **_The King cures the Problem._** Remember that our goal is to live with God in Heaven forever. But our problem of sin is getting in the way of that goal; God refuses to live with sinners! It's the only thing that is keeping us from Heaven. So, the King is going to get right to work on that problem. Everything in the ministry of the church is designed (or it should be!) to cure you of your sin.

  The first problem to solve is to define exactly what sin is. The King knows best here. We would love to redefine sin in our own way, because our limited and watered-down definitions are easy enough to solve with the least trouble to our sinful lives. But Jesus isn't satisfied. His standard is God's perfection itself.

> Be perfect, therefore, as your Heavenly Father is perfect. (Matthew 5:48)

> No one is good – except God alone. (Mark 10:18)

Now that he defines the standard, we can see how unreachable it is. This is humbling, but it's also a necessary step to our salvation. We know now that only Jesus is going to be able to get us to that high level of righteousness.

Next, he is going to show us just how much work we have to do in this area of sin. The scope of sin in our lives is terrifying. Little did we know, until we come into the King's presence and he demands our complete submission in all areas of our lives, just how far short of the mark we fall.

At this point we are helpless before the Judge of all the earth. Now he carefully prescribes the remedy for our sin – his Spirit, his power, his wisdom, his ways, his works. This will be a complete and successful program to change us from sinners to saints. We can do nothing else but trust him completely and follow him in whatever way he leads us. If we "grieve" him in any way and refuse to apply his remedy, however painful the discipline may be, we will not be cured. We can't afford to make any mistakes here. The King knows best what we need to be saved.

- ***The King takes care of all of our needs.*** One of the important aspects of a Kingdom is that the King takes care of his subjects. The good ones do, at any rate. Often we see a self-centered king or despot draining the resources of the land for his own selfish ends, and that perhaps makes us all the more determined to rule ourselves and refuse any king over us.

  In the case of the church, however, we can't afford *not* to have a King! First of all, he loves us – the Scripture says that he gave of himself for our sake. He's not the typical tyrant! He isn't King for his own sake, but for our sake. We now have a chance to live because of his care for us.

  Second, he puts us in touch with resources the like of which we have never dreamed.

  > Now to him who is able to do immeasurably more than all we ask or imagine, according to his power that is at work within us, to him be glory in the church and in Christ Jesus throughout all generations, for ever and ever! Amen. (Ephesians 3:20-21)

  The Treasures of Heaven – these satisfy the deepest longings of the human soul. They move mountains and raise valleys. They sustain God's people in the middle of the wilderness. They pick up the slack when the world disappoints us. Jesus has all the inheritance of God at his disposal, and he faithfully provides his subjects with whatever resources they will need on their journey from this world to the next. Prayer and faith get in touch with this treasure.

- ***The King leads the way and clears the path.*** We have a King who leads from the front. In war, you can tell which commanders really care about their troops. The ones who lead from the safety of their bunker that's way back in the rear – the troops have little respect for them. But the commander who is with them, leading them into battle, sharing in their privations and struggle – the troops will follow him anywhere. Jesus is like this.

Actually Jesus went one step further. He paved the entire way first, making it safe and easy for us to follow. The battle is not uncertain; he won it for us. Now he leads us through the lines to the same victory that he achieved in his own life. The way is made plain, and easy to take because of the work he did ahead of time to make it certain.

> Come to me, all you who are weary and burdened, and I will give you rest. Take my yoke upon you and learn from me, for I am gentle and humble in heart, and you will find rest for your souls. For my yoke is easy and my burden is light. (Matthew 11:28-30)

He leads us one step at a time, encouraging the faint-hearted, rebuking the cowardly and faithless, giving hope to those who struggle.

Now the discerning Christian will realize that he has a blessing from Heaven here that he must not pass up. He *must* take advantage of this King and what he will do for his people. It's not a burden to be ruled over by Jesus! It's life; it's the way to success. Running one's own life, by contrast, is a fatal mistake. The work of the King is crucial for our well-being.

How does Jesus rule?

Hopefully you can see where we are headed with this. The church has to be designed and run in such a way that *Christ rules over his people*. That's what his people need. The problem is that this doesn't happen by accident. Churches often organize in ways that obstruct the rule of Christ, and make it difficult if not impossible (humanly speaking – Christ will often let ignorant churches have their way!) for the King to rule.

It helps, therefore, to understand *how* Jesus intends to rule over us. There are three roads into the church that Jesus takes to rule and lead us. If we are careful to learn about these approaches, and keep them open and well-tended, the King will find no obstructions to his work and people will find it easy to follow his leading.

- *He rules through his Word* – The Church has various tools and methods for achieving the goal of bringing sinners into submission before God, but the most powerful one is the Word of God. Again, people use the Bible for all sorts of things – it lends itself to comfort, hope, encouragement, and other ministrations that appeal to the aching heart. But first and foremost the Bible is a manual for addressing man's central problem – his sin. Many have developed the ability to read around the sections that confront them as rebellious sinners and they head straight for the promises. However, that won't help them at all on Judgment Day. They must face the problem head-on. If you don't see yourself as a sinner, then you have not yet seen yourself, nor do you understand the purpose of the Bible.

The Bible is designed to do several things for us:

> *All Scripture is God-breathed and is useful for teaching, rebuking, correcting and training in righteousness, so that the man of God may be thoroughly equipped for every good work. (2 Timothy 3:16-17)*

Note what functions it serves us –

- **Teaching** – because we do not yet know what we need to know about either God, ourselves, our problem or the solution.
- **Rebuking** – because we keep sinning in many ways, and we need to face that fact and stop.
- **Correcting** – because we keep taking the wrong road and have to be continually shown the right way to go to follow Christ.
- **Training in righteousness** – because we have a long way to go before we are anywhere near the righteousness of Christ.

None of these functions appeal to our pride, all of them can be and are painful to go through, and yet they are necessary for every single person in the Church. In fact, if this isn't happening in a person's life when they study the Bible, they are using it to no purpose. You can, for example, use a geography book as a source of pretty pictures; but that's not its purpose. It has pretty pictures – but you are supposed to learn the principles of geography and master the knowledge. In the same way, people have their favorite passages underlined all through the Bible – usually the promises, almost never the humbling descriptions of their crippling sins and how to overcome them. You will never be saved from sin at that rate.

The old divines used to say that there are two main functions in Church – preaching and prayer. Whatever else there may be in your church (and unfortunately we sinners like to multiply functions in an effort to avoid or water down the two main ones) we need the preaching of the Word to convict us of our sin (John 16:8), and the ministry of prayer to appeal to God to change us from sinners to saints (Luke 18:13). In fact, if all you had in your church were these two functions, that would be all you really need to get ready for Heaven. The rest of what happens in churches nowadays is mostly just psychology and sociology and has no direct relevance to the task.

Christ, as the Head of the Church, has of course provided just what we need for the ministry of the Word in the Church.

> It was he who gave some to be Apostles, some to be prophets, some to be evangelists, and some to be pastors and teachers, to prepare God's people for works of service, so that the body of Christ may be built up until we all reach unity in the faith and in the knowledge of the Son of God and become mature, attaining to the whole measure of the fullness of Christ. (Ephesians 4:11-13)

The Apostles and Prophets gave us the Bible itself. The pastors and teachers take that Word and impress it on the hearers' lives. The process involved is *training* – a little-used concept in today's church, but desperately needed. The result is –

You were taught, with regard to your former way of life, to put off your old self, which is being corrupted by its deceitful desires; to be made new in the attitude of your minds; and to put on the new self, created to be like God in true righteousness and holiness. (Ephesians 4:22-24)

If the Word is faithfully taught as the King's will, and the members are listening and taking it to heart – in other words, they are changing from sinners to saints – then Jesus really does rule in that church.

- *He rules through his Spirit* – Jesus promised us that when he went back to Heaven he would send the Spirit to indwell us. It is conceivable that a person could read the Bible and learn its teachings, and yet not know the reality of God's spiritual world. But when a Christian has the Spirit of Christ in him, there is no way he can deny the reality of God – the Spirit brings him into the presence of God so that he can see God's glory, hear his voice, and love him.

The first step is to change the heart. The best passage that describes this event is in the Prophets.

> I will sprinkle clean water on you, and you will be clean; I will cleanse you from all your impurities and from all your idols. I will give you a new heart and put a new spirit in you; I will remove from you your heart of stone and give you a heart of flesh. And I will put my Spirit in you and move you to follow my decrees and be careful to keep my laws. (Ezekiel 36:25-27)

The first sign, therefore, of the presence of Christ is that a person's heart changes – and *that* is the basis of a changed life. He no longer loves sin or this world; he loves God and the next world. He is humble before God and obedient, ready to follow the Lord's will in his Word. He changes his lifestyle to please the Lord instead of his own lusts and desires. His heart fills with the fruit of the Spirit – a sure sign that there's spiritual life there.

> But the fruit of the Spirit is love, joy, peace, patience, kindness, goodness, faithfulness, gentleness and self-control. Against such things there is no law. Those who belong to Christ Jesus have crucified the sinful nature with its passions and desires. (Galatians 5:22-24)

Wise church leaders know about this. They know they can't change people's hearts – it's not their job to do that. Their duty is to preach the Word of Christ and then pray and wait for the Spirit to do the rest of the work. And they will make sure that they don't hinder the free operation of the gifts of the Spirit, because it's through these functions that the Lord develops his people's faith and life.

- ***He rules through Worship*** – To be exact, worship is the *result* of two things: preaching the Word as Christ's will, and the Spirit making God's spiritual world real to his people. But we can add worship as another aspect to the life of the church because it's a necessary outlet for the other two. Unfortunately, it *is* possible to bottle up the work of the Spirit in people's hearts by turning Christianity into a man-centered, introspective religion that puts the Spirit's fire out.

Worship is, as we've seen, humbling oneself before God. We will only truly worship God if we *know* him (the result of teaching the Word faithfully) and *see* him (the result of the Spirit opening our eyes to him). And we need to worship him for several reasons: ***first***, we see his glory, his overwhelming holiness, his profound wisdom, his love and faithfulness that knows no limits, his power that overwhelms. That sight will awe and terrify anybody, as the examples in the Bible show us clearly. ***Second***, we immediately see what we are in light of this God. Our sin is too much to bear, our ignorance is embarrassing and painful, our self-will and streak of independence is a dark stain in God's pure light. Who can stand before God in light of all that? ***Third***, we see how amazing God's love is in giving us a way of escape from our sin and weakness. The vision of Christ, if truly seen for what it is, is like a starving man seeing a feast laid out before him, or a dying man seeing the fountain of life. The treasures of Heaven are so appropriate for what I need! Why would Christ do such things for an unworthy sinner like me? ***Fourth***, we know exactly what we have to do – plead for that mercy and love of God in Christ given for us. We need this; we are desperate for this; we are reduced to helpless beggars, with nothing to offer God in return. But we are called by God to come, take and eat.

Hopefully you can get a sense of what true worship is from this picture. It can happen silently, it can happen in prayer, both individual and corporate, it can happen during the sermon or Sunday School lesson, it can happen in praise and song. But the reality of coming before God like this completes the circle and proves beyond all doubt that Jesus rules in his church.

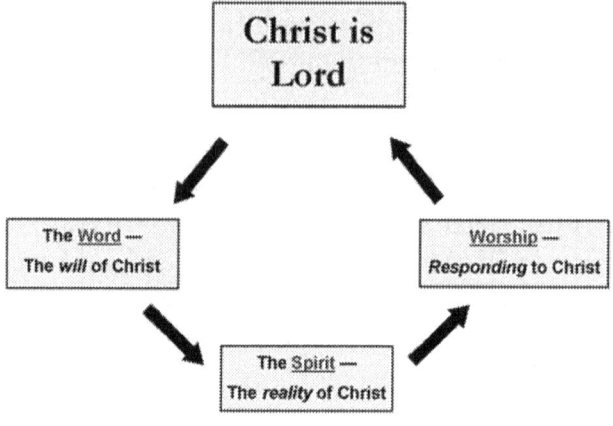

Christ rules in his church

The hierarchy of the Kingdom

The Israelites were infamous for their rebellion against God. What a shame – the very people that God chose to glorify him, and they dishonored him over and over in their history.

One fundamental problem that the Israelites had was the fact that they were supposed to follow a *spiritual* God. They couldn't see him, and so it was difficult to follow this invisible God. Or should we say, it was just too easy not to!

We share their problem. Jesus did indeed come in the flesh, but now he's back in Heaven. It often proves too difficult (or again, perhaps too easy *not* to!) to follow Jesus when we can't see him. If all we are following is a Name, it's not at all easy to pull everyone together and move in the same direction.

So, the Lord gave the Israelites a king – David. He successfully pulled the nation together and put them on track to glorifying God. One of the essential items to his reign was to set up a government that would carry out his orders across the land.

In the same way, Jesus has set up a government in his church. Not that he *couldn't* rule the church himself, but he has chosen instead to rule through his selected government officials. Their job is to carry out the Lord's orders and set up his Kingdom in his way.

There are three levels of government in Christ's Kingdom.

- *First*, the **Apostles and Prophets** got their authority from God himself. Their duty was more than simply to wander around the world preaching and starting churches. God gave them the **Word**, they wrote it down, and they passed it on to us. We now possess the Word of God by their efforts. That's why the work of the Prophets and Apostles is so fundamental to the work of the Church.

> Consequently, you are no longer foreigners and aliens, but fellow citizens with God's people and members of God's household, ***built on the foundation of the Apostles and Prophets,*** with Christ Jesus himself as the chief cornerstone. (Ephesians 2:19-20)

We honor that authority by learning and doing what they passed on to us from Christ. These are the very words of God. In other words (in case it hasn't hit you yet) *we do not deviate from the truth of the Bible.* We are not free to add to it or subtract from it. It is true just as it stands. It doesn't need our present culture to improve it. It is truth for all ages, all people everywhere, just as it reads. People who would water down or do away with passages in the Bible are enemies of Christ – and the church needs to identify them as such.

This Word – both Old and New Testaments – is what God has given his church through all ages to be saved from sin and death. It is perfectly adequate to do that job. It is the full statement of our faith and practice; we need nothing else for the purpose. And with the work of the Spirit, all of God's people can understand its message and be saved – they need nothing else but the Word of God. [2]

- *Second*, **pastors and teachers** are also assigned to their jobs – Christ gave these functions to the Church for her growth and well-being. Where did we get the notion that these functions in the church are hired positions? To treat a pastor or teacher in Christ's church as an employee is to reject Christ's authority. Pastors usually get a "paycheck," but that doesn't make the shepherd an employee of the sheep – such an idea is absurd. Pastors and teachers are Christ's workers, shepherds assigned to the job of caring for Christ's flock. The "pay" that a pastor receives is compensation for his hard work for the flock, and imposed on that flock by the Lord of the Church.

> The elders who direct the affairs of the church well are worthy of double honor, especially those whose work is preaching and teaching. For the Scripture says, "Do not muzzle the ox while it is treading out the grain," and "The worker deserves his wages." (1 Timothy 5:17-18)

Shepherds are answerable to the Chief Shepherd. They are to do the job he gave them to do, as he describes it in his Word. To hold them responsible to do what church members dream up as a replacement for God's job description in the Bible is to shackle them with trivia that prevents them from doing *Christ's* will.

> So the Twelve gathered all the disciples together and said, "It would not be right for us to neglect the

---

[2] A fascinating example of Jesus "doing as his father David had done" is found in the Gospels that show us Christ choosing his disciples. He was literally collecting the "materials" for the spiritual Temple he is building; they are the "foundation" that he would build his church upon. See Matthew 4:18-22.

ministry of the Word of God in order to wait on tables. Brothers, choose seven men from among you who are known to be full of the Spirit and wisdom. We will turn this responsibility over to them and will give our attention to prayer and the ministry of the Word." (Acts 6:2-4)

Their allegiance and obedience is *upward* in the hierarchy, to Christ – their duties downward to the flock.

> Be shepherds of God's flock that is under your care, serving as overseers – not because you must, but because you are willing, as God wants you to be; not greedy for money, but eager to serve; not lording it over those entrusted to you, but being examples to the flock. And when the Chief Shepherd appears, you will receive the crown of glory that will never fade away. (1 Peter 5:1-4)

The authority of a leader is not an empty concept. He has the right and the duty to use the Word of God boldly in the church – applying it to people's hearts as necessary. If he shies away from his duty to confront sinners with their sin, he isn't doing them any favors and he is opening up the whole church to confusion about how serious sin is. And if he beats the sheep, the Chief Shepherd is going to have harsh words for him. So at times he has to be firm and confrontational, and at other times gentle and compassionate. His goal at all times, however, is to lead the flock to salvation in Christ. We *have* to take them seriously – they are Christ's representatives.

> I will give you the keys of the kingdom of Heaven; whatever you bind on earth will be bound in Heaven, and whatever you loose on earth will be loosed in Heaven. (Matthew 16:19)

> This is why I write these things when I am absent, that when I come I may not have to be harsh in my use of authority – the authority the Lord gave me for building you up, not for tearing you down. (2 Corinthians 13:10)

The leaders of the church are responsible for *teaching* and *discipline*. They are to use the Word alone for teaching; as we've seen, God's people need only God's Word, and all of God's Word, to be saved and prepared for Heaven. The leaders are responsible to become well-trained in the Bible so that they can give the flock what it needs.

> Therefore every teacher of the Law who has been instructed about the kingdom of Heaven is like the owner of a house who brings out of his storeroom new treasures as well as old. (Matthew 13:52)

> Do your best to present yourself to God as one approved, a workman who does not need to be ashamed and who correctly handles the word of truth. (2 Timothy 2:15)

Discipline involves many things – correcting troublemakers in the church is only one of its aspects. Perhaps if you think of the military you will begin to appreciate its fuller meaning. In order to prepare soldiers for battle, the officers make the recruits drill and practice and drill and practice until they can do it in their sleep! This continual training is for a purpose: on the battlefield, a soldier has to the *right* thing *immediately*, or he will die. There is no time to study in the middle of a battle. The right action has to be instinct. In the same way, the leaders of the church must train the members in the truths and practice of Christianity so that, when the time comes and we are called upon to defend ourselves against the enemy, we also will do the right thing without hesitation or doubt.

Leaders are not to be subject to the whims of the discontents of the flock, because in every group there are those who will target the leaders to take the spotlight off themselves. They demand that the leader do their will, and in the process create no end of confusion and trouble.

> Do not entertain an accusation against an elder unless it is brought by two or three witnesses. (1 Timothy 5:19)

An elder who goes bad is a public matter, and the church should proceed carefully to rebuke an elder. Most of the complaints against leaders, however, come from ignorance, rebellion, and the need for a scapegoat – and should be dismissed as such. It's easy to hurl accusations against the leaders when you're sitting in the back row, but they are almost never true. Moses had continual complaints and accusations thrown against him, all undeserved. Leaders carry burdens that the members know little about – not only the commands from the Lord about things that must be done in the ministry of the church, but the problems of all the members of the church weigh on them also. Criticisms from ignorant members only make things harder for them.

> Obey your leaders and submit to their authority. They keep watch over you as men who must give an account. Obey them so that their work will be a joy, not a burden, for that would be of no advantage to you. (Hebrews 13:17)

- **Third**, Christ has given **spiritual gifts** to various members of the church. In today's churches, the subject of spiritual gifts is little understood and almost never explored. Preachers are always hammering on the subject – "everyone has a gift they should be using" – but members, though willing, have no idea how to proceed in even identifying their gift, let alone using it. And then you often have that insecure pastor who would really rather you *didn't* use your gift because it would take away from his own power and influence in the church!

The gifts are designed to distribute Christ's grace to the flock. They are channels through which the King influences and blesses his subjects from Heaven. The gifts that Christ gives to the church [3] are listed in Romans 12:6-8, 1 Corinthians 12:8-10, Ephesians 4:11, and 1 Peter 4:10-11. A spiritual gift brings others into the presence of Christ. It makes the spiritual world of God more real to people so that they are confronted, encouraged, enabled with the presence of God in their lives. It aids in worship, the life of faith, seeing the truth of the Word, and obedient living. As you can see, the jobs of "pastor" and "teacher" are not the only means that Christ spiritually enriches his flock. It's critical for the spiritual well-being of the flock that every member does his duty and helps build Christ's Kingdom.

Submitting to the King

A church will succeed only if it recognizes the rule of Christ over it. Jesus is King; the church members need him desperately. They can't live without him and the things he can do for them and give them.

But this also means that they must recognize the system of authority that Christ has set up in the church. The government of the church is specifically designed to carry out the will of Christ, and dispense his resources among his people. Submission to authority is a hallmark of a successful church. We are

---

[3] This brings up an important point – you can't claim that every natural skill you might have is a "spiritual gift." Christ knows what his church needs, and he enables the bearer of the spiritual gift to do the work he is after. You may have a natural artistic ability; but "art" is not one of the spiritual gifts. His Word, remember, reveals the truth to us and directs the affairs of the church, not our opinions or feelings.

commanded to submit to the church authority, because only in this way will we get in touch with the King himself. If we rebel against church authority, we are actually separating ourselves from the King. He hates that! Not only are we refusing to follow the very avenues to spiritual life and growth, we are falling back to our original problem of sin – rebellion against God, and the suffering and death that comes as a result.

This of course requires two things: *first*, that the church leadership extend Christ's rule over the group (not their own!), and *second*, that the members recognize that Christ rules over them by means of the leadership and functions of the church. That's why we said, at the beginning, that the church is a perfect fit: the good church gives people what they really need from Jesus, and people come to a good church because they know they're getting in touch with Christ himself.

The church will never work if there isn't an attitude of submission to authority. This principle is foundational to the life and success of any church. If people are willing to recognize and submit to Christ's authority over them (in all of its forms), then they will be pleasing to God and everyone will achieve their goal of reaching Heaven.

The Church – an agent of change

I tell you the truth, unless you change and become like little children, you will never enter the kingdom of Heaven. (Matthew 18:3)

When we consider what God has done for us in the past, what he's doing now, and what he will do for us in the future, it's truly astonishing. It isn't anything like what we are used to in this world. The wealthy and powerful will die and become nothing in the end; God's people, often despised and forsaken in this world, will assume their places beside Christ in eternity and rule the universe.

> He raises the poor from the dust and lifts the needy from the ash heap; he seats them with princes and has them inherit a throne of honor. (1 Samuel 2:8)

But I'm not sure this truth has hit us yet. We know what it's like to change jobs, or leave our parents and get married and have our own families. We have all experienced some sort of change in our lives. But the jump from this world to the next, from our position here to an unimaginable position in Heaven with God – that is something we little understand and perhaps think little about. It will be *shocking*, the difference between life here and life there. There's nothing we've experienced so far that will get us ready for that change.

The reason I believe that we have thought so little about this change is because we are doing hardly anything to get ready for it. If we truly understood what was coming, we would be making *some* sort of preparations for the change. We would understand that *we must change* in order to be ready for Heaven. We can't go there as we are now. For several reasons that we want to look at here, we are really not ready to go yet. There's a lot of work to be done before the Lord will move us to our new home.

What is our goal?

Our goal is to live with God, plain and simple. Adam was created to live with God (the greatest blessing of all!) but he passed up his chance when he chose to live on his own. We Christians have another chance to reconcile with God and live with him; that's the promise that God has made us, his people. Christ's entire mission was to carry out that goal.

And if that's our goal, then we have a couple of problems facing us right away.

- *First*, we are sinners – and no sinners are allowed into Heaven. Only a righteous and holy people will live with a righteous and holy God. The problem is that God's standards are terrifyingly sharp – not a single sin, not a single rebellious thought, will be allowed into his world. Not only must we be totally righteous, but we must remain that way forever.

- *Second*, God and Heaven are spiritual, and we are not. We are physical and we know only what our senses tell us. Our hearts, unfortunately, are infatuated with this world; we live for it, we love it, and we don't want to lose it. So, we are in a bad position to enter a world that we can't understand and won't appreciate.

The first duty of a serious Christian is to come to grips with these two problems. Of course, if he doesn't care about Heaven, he won't bother with these problems; in fact, they won't be any problem to him. He will only use a church to make his life in this physical world more comfortable. But if Heaven is important to him, these problems will suddenly appear as unwelcome obstacles blocking the way in his journey to Paradise.

We must change

The point, then, is to realize that *we are not yet what we ought to be.* This is a fundamental aspect of a Christian's mentality. Why do believers think that they've done everything that they need to do when they first got converted? The truth is that we have just begun the journey to Heaven. There is a lot to do to get ready. Getting converted simply turned our steps from earth to Heaven. Christians aren't immediately taken to be with God at conversion; instead, they are now being prepared and protected for the journey there.

> I have given them your Word and the world has hated them, for they are not of the world any more than I am of the world. My prayer is not that you take them out of the world but that you protect them from the evil one. They are not of the world, even as I am not of it. Sanctify them by the truth; your Word is truth. (John 17:14-17)

Jesus is the Perfect Man; the Scripture says that God was "pleased" only with his Son. So if we ever hope to enter Heaven, our job now, as Christians, is to change and become conformed to the image of Christ.

> And we, who with unveiled faces all reflect the Lord's glory, are being transformed into his likeness with ever-increasing glory, which comes from the Lord, who is the Spirit. (2 Corinthians 3:18)

A Church for Christians – an agent of change

People hate to change, particularly adults. They feel that they've invested a lot of time and energy becoming who they are, and pride won't let them admit that they are not what they should be. And in church, about the only people there who will accept the fact that they must change are the children. The adults will smile and tell you that they appreciated your lesson or sermon, but they have no intention of doing what you told them. If you push them, they get angry and fight, and perhaps will even leave the church. But *change* is not an option for them, unfortunately.

This is why Jesus told his disciples that they must become like little children.

> I tell you the truth, unless you change and become like little children, you will never enter the kingdom of Heaven. Therefore, whoever humbles himself like this child is the greatest in the kingdom of Heaven. (Matthew 18:3-4)

Jesus has no time for arrogant adults. If people don't want to change into his image, then he'll pick up and move off to another spot and work with someone else. He will write "Ichabod" over the door of that obstinate church and leave. He knows, even if we don't, the severe requirements of Heaven, and how unsuited we are to live there in our present state. And he also knows that church-goers who don't want to prepare for Heaven are simply playing games at church; they may as well stay at home, or transfer their membership to some civic club.

How much do we need to change? There's a simple test that you can take.

- ***Are you like Christ?*** Are you wholly taken up with God, night and day? Do you work continuously for the Kingdom of God? Are all your thoughts and actions pure and righteous, to the extent that the Law of God would have no problem with you? Is God pleased with you in every way – a faithful son, a fearless warrior against the enemy, full of wisdom and truth?

- ***Do you know anything about what life is like in Heaven?*** Do you know its language, its customs, its laws? Do you know what the angels are doing there – are you ready to command and lead them in their work? Do you know what the house of God is like – can you take advantage of its furniture, its layout, its treasures, in your work there? Do you know what it's like to stand before God and give him the service that is due him? Do you understand why your physical world would be so out of place there in Heaven?

Jesus, the perfect Son of God, is like this. But if this doesn't describe you, then you are not yet ready to live with God. You have a lot of changing to do.

One of the greatest saints of the Bible had a humble attitude when it came to thinking about Heaven. Paul, known as the greatest of the Apostles, certainly had a lot to recommend him to us. He wrote much of the New Testament. He understood the mysteries of the Gospel, and was assigned the huge task of taking it to the Gentiles – a job that his Jewish brethren weren't ready to do. His insight and wisdom and holy life even impressed the other Apostles, like Peter (see 2 Peter 3:16).

If ever a man knew Christ and the way to Heaven, Paul certainly should have. If there was ever a saint who could claim, at any point along the way, that he was ready for Heaven, Paul ought to be that man. Yet we read an astonishing admission on his part that *he was not yet what he needed to be for that transition!*

I want to know Christ and the power of his resurrection and the fellowship of sharing in his sufferings, becoming like him in his death, and so, somehow, to attain to the resurrection from the dead. *Not that I have already obtained all this, or have already been made perfect*, but I press on to take hold of that for which Christ Jesus took hold of me. Brothers, *I do not consider myself yet to have taken hold of it*. But one thing I do: Forgetting what is behind and straining toward what is ahead, I press on toward the goal to win the prize for which God has called me Heavenward in Christ Jesus. All of us who are mature should take such a view of things. And if on some point you think differently, that too God will make clear to you. (Philippians 3:10-15)

The great Paul, the mature Paul who has led so many others to Christ and started churches around the Roman Empire, humbles himself like a child and admits of his need to *change*. And this wasn't just a show of humility; he truly felt his great need to know more about Christ – because Christ is infinite. Paul could see a truly infinite horizon in front of him, something he couldn't possibly hope to achieve on his own. He longed to plunge into that expanding world with all his soul, to immerse himself more and more in the infinite grace and joy of Christ. We who don't understand his vision of the greatness of Christ, Paul pities. We who do understand will follow Paul into that new world at whatever cost.

A spiritual hospital

Many people go to church thinking that they've already attained God's goals. Change is the last thing on their minds! They are there to enjoy themselves, to enjoy the show, to socialize, to make friends, to do their religious duty and go home satisfied that they obeyed God by going to church.

In other words, these people think, for all practical purposes, that they are perfect. At least perfect enough to satisfy God's requirements for getting into Heaven. They aren't there to change, they will refuse to change, they don't even want to think about changing. They would never admit to all this, of course, but their actions speak louder than their words. If you press them about the need to be holy, they will go along with the program as long as you limit the areas of change to certain "safe" areas that they are willing to give up anyway (*"I don't drink, I don't chew, don't go out with girls who do!"*) But to seriously face the fact that they are *sinners*, and earthly-minded, and not at all fit to live with God without some serious character changes – don't even waste your breath. They are not willing to go to that extent; they will leave first and find a more comfortable church to attend.

Let them go. There are, unfortunately, many churches tailor-made to "minister" to this kind of person. Not every church understands – or perhaps we should say, it's a rare church that understands – the Mission. Most churches have some sort of mission statement, and it's disheartening to read some of them. They are there to do all sorts of things for their members, but rarely do we read about solving spiritual problems.

Christ's church is a spiritual hospital. **We are here to fix the two problems that face all of mankind.** As soon as we walk in the door, we are telling everyone in the church that we are spiritually sick, we are bogged down with this world, and we need Christ's medicine to save us. We announce to everyone that we need help; that's why we're there. The leaders of the church

A Church for Christians – an agent of change

take us under their wing for that purpose.[4] The resources of the church are designed to help you change from a sinner to a saint, and from a citizen of earth to a citizen of Heaven. Becoming a church member is like checking yourself into a hospital.

If people don't take advantage of what the church is designed to do, they are wasting their time and everyone else's time. In fact, they will probably be more of a problem than anything, since they're going to spend their time resisting the efforts of the church to change them. The wise Christian comes to church to change, not to remain the same. And the changes that he has to undergo will be extensive, life-changing, and profound. He will need all sorts of things that the church is designed to give him. When a Christian understands this, and the church understands this, then we can accomplish our goal effectively to God's glory.

If this is the purpose of church – to help us change into what God wants us to be – then why do so many people resist the church's ministry when it tries to help them? Our modern churches are so frightened by the consumer attitude of its members that leaders are afraid to say anything at all critical about people! The Bible commands us to rebuke the saints when necessary about their sin, but it's a rare pastor or elder who will even consider doing such a thing to a church member. It will certainly start a war if he dares to rebuke someone! Most church splits and wars happen because someone took offense at a simple rebuke from a leader who was just doing his duty. The modern churchgoer just will not tolerate being told that he or she is wrong about anything and needs to change.

---

[4] The leaders are there to change too. If they themselves don't practice what they teach the sheep, they can't expect to escape God's displeasure just because they were leaders. See 1 Corinthians 9:27.

This is so foolish. It only shows the heart of those who refuse to change. And it cripples the work of the leaders so that they can't do their job.

> He who listens to a life-giving rebuke will be at home among the wise. He who ignores discipline despises himself, but whoever heeds correction gains understanding. (Proverbs 15:31-32)

Instead, we've turned church into an amusement center, with leaders playing the role of salesmen and entertainers, just to keep people interested enough to come back every Sunday. Say one word about their sin, however, and the room would become empty overnight. We can't get anywhere with the Mission when people are like that. God will have nothing good to say about us when we're so rebellious against his Word. What will our generation say, on Judgment Day, when they have so little to show for their work? How little we were able to do because people were too proud to admit that they needed help!

Our attitude has to change. We have to be so desperate about getting into Heaven that we will submit ourselves to the ministry of the church – *whatever it takes*. It's like going to a doctor for surgery. If you don't want him to touch you, why did you go? Of course it will hurt; but it's for your good, so that you will live. If you turn away from the church because you don't want to be told about your sin, and you don't want to change, then why go in the first place? You may as well just stay home and die! Because that's exactly what's going to happen to you if you don't get some help somewhere.

Let's look at several areas in which the Christian needs to change.

- ***There are things that we need to learn.*** "The man who thinks he knows something does not yet know as he ought to know." (1 Corinthians 8:2) The new Christian is like a new-born baby. He is now aware of God and the spiritual world. A brand-new mode of existence has opened up before him that he wasn't even aware of before. The initial rush of information about God and salvation in the Lord Jesus thrills the new believer.

But just as a baby grows up and continues to learn, so must the Christian. Here is where we unfortunately stumble in our spiritual walk, particularly the adults. Since we've spent a life-time of learning the world's ways, we are done with learning. Even though we may still be spiritual infants, knowing very little about God and Heaven, we fall back on our worldly knowledge and years of experience and consider ourselves quite mature. In other words, we take our *physical* maturity as *spiritual* maturity – yet the two don't coincide at all.

This is why Paul rebuked the spiritually ignorant of his day in this passage in Corinthians. Some of the worst trouble-makers in the church are those who think they know what's going on, yet they are still spiritual infants – they actually know very little about spiritual matters. Our great need is to *grow* in the knowledge of the Lord Jesus, not remain ignorant.

> But grow in the grace and knowledge of our Lord and Savior Jesus Christ. (2 Peter 3:18)

The spiritual world of God is enormous – actually as infinite as he is. The Kingdom of God – what is happening there, our duties there, its economy and organization, its growth on earth and its heavenly powers – is beyond what any earthly kingdom can boast. There is no end of the things that we can learn, and need to learn, in order to take our places as responsible citizens of this new world. The mind of man isn't capable of comprehending the enormity and complexity of God's world. Why, then, do we think we already know what we need to know about God when we are such spiritual infants?

The writer of Hebrews had to point out to his readers that they weren't ready yet to follow him into the deeper matters of the faith.

> We have much to say about this, but it is hard to explain because you are slow to learn. In fact, though by this time you ought to be teachers, you need someone to teach you the elementary truths of God's word all over again. You need milk, not solid food! (Hebrews 5:11-12)

And our modern Christians would, unfortunately, fall under the same rebuke. Most people in churches don't know much about Jesus – except the simplistic sermons about him being a Savior who loves them. They know almost nothing about the Old Testament, though it makes up three-fourths of their Bibles. Many of them can't even find the books of the Bible! Yet these same people will argue with pastors and teachers over doctrine and church policy as if they were experts in the field. Unfortunately they are more of an obstacle to church work, not a help, because of their ignorance.

The means of growing in knowledge is the Bible itself – which is another way you can tell whether someone is in "growing mode." The Bible is our *means of spiritual growth*; a Christian has to be serious about learning – from the Bible itself – if he has any hope of maturing in the faith.

> But his delight is in the Law of the LORD, and on his Law he meditates day and night. He is like a tree planted by streams of water, which yields its fruit in season and whose leaf does not wither. Whatever he does prospers. (Psalm 1:2-3)

> Like newborn babies, crave pure spiritual milk, so that by it you may grow up in your salvation, now that you have tasted that the Lord is good. (1 Peter 2:2-3)

How much is there to learn? If you consider that the Bible is actually a manual for the Kingdom of God, you might get a better idea of the scope of the task before us. For example, any responsible citizen of our country knows that he or she has to learn at least some things about our culture, our political system, our local government's rules and regulations, in order to get along well. And if he wants to get more involved in society than just flipping hamburgers – like become a teacher or mayor or doctor – he must learn a great deal more about the world around him. The more that we are involved with our society, the more we must learn. The same goes for God's Kingdom: the more you want to be involved with God, the more you must learn about him and his world.

God's Kingdom is an enormous, complex world that is far bigger than we are. If we are content to "flip hamburgers" spiritually – that is, exist on a day-to-day basis doing little more than opening our mouths like babies and expecting someone to feed us, and expecting someone else to clean up our messes that we created – then we will be content to remain ignorant of almost everything about God. But then neither will he use us for anything important! If we want to become more involved in his Kingdom and take responsible positions and bring him glory, then we have a lot of learning to do. We have to learn enough to become proficient in the area of expertise that he assigns to us.

God's world consists of government, business, education, health services, utilities, child care, the military – all the same kinds of elements that are in our world. But none of these elements match their counterparts in this physical world. They are on a spiritual plane; they will require a complete re-education on our part. Those who are good at this world's skills will find themselves hopelessly out-of-place and ineffectual in God's world. All the materials there are spiritual, the principles and guidelines are spiritual, the goals are spiritual. It needs skilled laborers, *not* untrained volunteers, who know how to work in a new kind of Kingdom.

> It was he who gave some to be Apostles, some to be Prophets, some to be evangelists, and some to be pastors and teachers, to prepare God's people for works of service, so that the body of Christ may be built up until we all reach unity in the faith and in the knowledge of the Son of God and become mature, attaining to the whole measure of the fullness of Christ. (Ephesians 4:11-13)

We can't afford to ignore this re-education effort in the church. Too many so-called Christians sit back in the church and resist all attempts to teach them anything; what little they already know is good enough for them. What they don't realize is that the Enemy is busy gathering up ignorant souls like them and putting them safely away in cults and other spiritual dead-ends. Only the *learner* in church will escape his devastating work among today's lazy Christians.

> Then we will no longer be infants, tossed back and forth by the waves, and blown here and there by every wind of teaching and by the cunning and craftiness of men in their deceitful scheming. Instead, speaking the truth in love, we will in all things grow up into him who is the Head, that is, Christ. From him the whole body, joined and held together by every supporting ligament, grows and builds itself up in love, as each part does its work. (Ephesians 4:14-16)

Unfortunately most church services are so immature, educationally speaking, that there really isn't much difference between them and a kindergarten class. It's a wonder to me that intelligent people keep going. "Fun" and rowdy sing-alongs, pictures and videos, games and parties and "celebrations," and messages that aren't any deeper than "Jesus loves me, this I know, for the Bible tells me so." Well, that's true – but the ultimate aim for a Christian is not to stay forever in kindergarten!

It's important to realize that the church is *designed* to educate you; that's one of its main functions. The purpose of preaching and teaching is to get data into your head. It's nothing other than God's classroom, and we are his students getting ready to take our places as responsible citizens in his Kingdom. It takes a lot of discipline, a lot of study, and a lot of time and effort, to reach our goal. The church has to organize itself to educate its people, and the members have to dig in and learn. Only when both have this mentality will the church achieve its Mission.

- ***We have to become holy.*** Holiness is not the same as righteousness; many people are confused about this. Righteousness, as we will see, is a purity of heart that will not walk in the ways of sin. But holiness is one step higher than that. Holiness is being completely devoted to God.

    > Enoch walked with God; then he was no more, because God took him away. (Genesis 5:24)

    The Lord instructed the Israelites to treat the articles in the Temple with great respect – the altars, the wash-basins and lampstands, and everything else that was used for God's service. These things were "set apart" for God's use, and couldn't be used for common purposes. This idea of being "set apart" is the meaning of the word "holy" in Hebrew.

    In the same way, Christians have been "set apart" for God's use, as soon as the sanctifying Holy Spirit entered their hearts.

> Having believed, you were marked in him with a seal, the promised Holy Spirit, who is a deposit guaranteeing our inheritance until the redemption of those who are God's possession – to the praise of his glory. (Ephesians 1:13-14)

We are no longer our own. We are God's servants, designed and called to glorify him and work in his Kingdom.

> But now that you have been set free from sin and have become slaves to God, the benefit you reap leads to holiness, and the result is eternal life. (Romans 6:22)

In other words, Christianity is not something that you do for an hour each week on Sundays. It's a 24/7 job. The purpose of prayer, for example, is to check in with God on a regular basis and get his orders for the day. The purpose of studying the Word is to get more familiar with his Kingdom and learn his ways and works, so that you can live effectively in his spiritual Kingdom. The purpose of fellowship is to get to know your eternal family better, and start working out those kinks in your character that make love for others difficult for you to do.

> And whatever you do, whether in word or deed, do it all in the name of the Lord Jesus, giving thanks to God the Father through him. (Colossians 3:17)

We have embarked on a new life, into a new world. This world is dominated by the presence of

God. It isn't going to be anything like the old physical existence. And there's no turning back now.

> No one who puts his hand to the plow and looks back is fit for service in the kingdom of God. (Luke 9:62)

Yes, a life like this is strange, and it's very demanding – especially since we still have one foot in this old world. But the church is designed to help you get used to God's world, and living in the presence of God. We have all been set apart for God; so when we get together, we can let our guard down and share what we have in common – God – knowing that our neighbor, who has as much at stake here as we do, will help us.

> But you are a chosen people, a royal priesthood, a holy nation, a people belonging to God, that you may declare the praises of him who called you out of darkness into his wonderful light. (1 Peter 2:9)

This isn't going to be something that any of us know how to do at the beginning of our spiritual walk. The new-born Christian wants to please God and live for him, but – like an infant – he doesn't know how yet. Remember that God's world is enormous and complex; just to *learn* what is involved in living for God is a huge task in front of us! After we learn, however, we have to start incorporating these principles into our lives, and that will take time and much practice and training. The Old Testament tells us that we, like the boy Samuel, are living in God's house now. We have to learn the house rules, and God's expectations and ways, and arrange our lives to conform to his Kingdom.

> In him the whole building is joined together and rises to become a holy Temple in the Lord. And in him you too are being built together to become a dwelling in which God lives by his Spirit. (Ephesians 2:21-22)

- ***We must crucify our sin.*** This is where righteousness comes in. And this is, unfortunately, a sensitive area for us – it's the very problem that alienated us from God in the first place. In fact, our sin is so deeply rooted in our natures that it will be like having heart surgery to get it out of us. It will take drastic measures.

Sin – which is rebellion against God's rule over us – is the first and only problem of mankind. All other problems stem from this one. If we would have obeyed God completely, he would have blessed us and there would be no such things as death and suffering in our world. If you think about this for a while, you will hopefully see how destructive and horrific sin must be, to be the cause of all the chaos and ills of mankind.

Even the smallest sin is lethal to our spirits. The saints who understand this will spare no effort to root all sin out of their lives. It's like an enemy that is still within the walls of the city, lurking for the right opportunity to stab us in the back in the dark.

> Search me, O God, and know my heart; test me and know my anxious thoughts. See if

there is any offensive way in me, and lead me in the way everlasting. (Psalm 139:23-24)

Needless to say, we can't stay in sin any longer if we hope to be a part of God's new Kingdom. If *one* sin brought the entire world down in ruin (Genesis 3), then you can be sure that God will not allow even a single sin in Heaven. It has to be all washed away. Our devotion to God, our obedience to him and his will, has to be so perfect that – millions of eons from now – there still won't be even the idea of rebellion against him.

As you can see, there is much to do here. The fact is that, right now, we think about God and obey him *so little* that the thought of us being good citizens of Heaven is a laugh. The angels, who live before God and "serve him day and night," wonder what has to be done to our natures to get us up to even their level, let alone closer to the throne of glory as a member of the Family.

Let's be clear about something first. When a person becomes a Christian, he is *righteous* in God's eyes. In our eyes he most certainly isn't, but what God sees is the Spirit of Christ in this person's heart – and where Christ is, there is his righteousness. He's a covering over our souls; when the destroying angel flies over looking for sinners, Christ protects us with his righteousness and turns the destroyer away from us. We are his now, and the Law can't punish us.

But there's still this matter of our sinful natures. Underneath that protective covering of Christ's righteousness is our willful, rebellious, perverted heart and mind that still need a great deal of cleansing. There is much to change here. We aren't usually aware of just how much is there until the right circumstances come along and uncover what we really are inside. Sex, money and politics – which, unfortunately, are constant issues even in the church – will often bring out the worst in us. Then we see these "holy" church members turn into greedy, hateful, perverted monsters overnight.

That's why there are so many commands in the letters of the Apostles to address this issue of living righteous lives.

> Put to death, therefore, whatever belongs to your earthly nature: sexual immorality, impurity, lust, evil desires and greed, which is idolatry. Because of these, the wrath of God is coming. You used to walk in these ways, in the life you once lived. But now you must rid yourselves of all such things as these: anger, rage, malice, slander, and filthy language from your lips. Do not lie to each other, since you have taken off your old self with its practices and have put on the new self, which is being renewed in knowledge in the image of its Creator. (Colossians 3:5-10)

> Live such good lives among the pagans that, though they accuse you of doing wrong, they may see your good deeds and glorify God on the day he visits us. (1 Peter 2:12)

We just don't have room to do more than give a couple of examples here. The Apostles never assume that, since you now have the righteousness of Christ, then you don't have anything to work on. They continually press the urgency of getting your outward life to match your inward spiritual standing in Christ. In other words, now that you have been made one with the Righteous Christ, *live like it* – and it will take a lot of time and effort to do this.

On the other hand, you're wasting your time if you think you can pull this off by your own effort. You couldn't do it before you became a Christian, and you can't do it now, either. The key is to rely on Christ's Spirit that now lives in you. He is there to give you the power to overcome your sinful nature. You have to learn to follow the Spirit, and be led by him, as he changes you from sinner to saint.

> So I say, live by the Spirit, and you will not gratify the desires of the sinful nature … Since we live by the Spirit, let us keep in step with the Spirit. (Galatians 5:16, 25)

When we are finally showing the fruit of the Spirit in our lives – love, joy, peace, patience, kindness, goodness, faithfulness, and self-control – even in the fires of trial and conflict, then we can say that we are changing for the better.

The church is designed to help you address your problem of sin. The Bible's teaching aims primarily at curing our sin.

> Therefore, get rid of all moral filth and the evil that is so prevalent and humbly accept the word planted in you, which can save you. Do not merely listen to the Word, and so deceive yourselves. Do what it says. Anyone who listens to the Word but does not do what it says

is like a man who looks at his face in a mirror and, after looking at himself, goes away and immediately forgets what he looks like. But the man who looks intently into the perfect Law that gives freedom, and continues to do this, not forgetting what he has heard, but doing it – he will be blessed in what he does. (James 1:21-25)

And the church, because it has the resources to address the problem of sin, is the perfect place to begin working on restoring our relationship to God and man. To God, the King under whom we learn obedience and service; and to man, our brother whom we must love and help. If we don't learn it here – and unfortunately the church often turns into a battleground where the exact opposite happens! – then where will we learn righteousness? Certainly not in the world!

- ***We have to cut our ties with this world.*** Little do we realize how tied to this world we really are. We are children of our age. We think the way we've been trained to think; we share the same values as our neighbors; we fill our lives with the goods and pleasures of the world. If we aren't ready to live in Heaven, it's primarily because we are so in love with our life here.

    We've seen the great need for getting ready for Heaven; it's a strange world, and there are realities there that we want to get used to now if we hope to fit in on our arrival and take advantage of them. But while there's that hope in front of us, there's another reality behind us that is driving us to change – immediately. There is the urgency of war behind us.

> But the day of the Lord will come like a thief. The heavens will disappear with a roar; the elements will be destroyed by fire, and the earth and everything in it will be laid bare. Since everything will be destroyed in this way, what kind of people ought you to be? You ought to live holy and godly lives as you look forward to the day of God and speed its coming. That day will bring about the destruction of the heavens by fire, and the elements will melt in the heat. But in keeping with his promise we are looking forward to a new Heaven and a new earth, the home of righteousness. So then, dear friends, since you are looking forward to this, make every effort to be found spotless, blameless and at peace with him. (2 Peter 3:10-14)

God is going to destroy this world. When will he do this? We don't know, but it's a certainty. We don't want to be here when it happens.

But for some reason, many Christians are quite satisfied with this world and they are giving little or no thought to leaving it. Even the leadership caters to this attitude: their messages focus on how to be a successful Christian businessman, or housewife, or politician. There's a hurricane on the horizon, and everyone is settling down on the beach for a picnic!

The urgency of the Mission of the church is to get people out of this world. This will involve, again, a lot of effort and time. We are so used to this world that it's going to be a difficult matter to start thinking in terms of Heaven. For example, the rich young ruler came to Jesus thinking that he was ready for Heaven. He found out, however, that he wasn't willing to leave this world with its riches and comforts. (Luke 18:18-23)

This world is nothing but a trap to keep us away from God. It's time to cut your ties with it.

> Do not conform any longer to the pattern of this world, but be transformed by the renewing of your mind. Then you will be able to test and approve what God's will is – his good, pleasing and perfect will. (Romans 12:2)

> Do not love the world or anything in the world. If anyone loves the world, the love of the Father is not in him. For everything in the world – the cravings of sinful man, the lust of his eyes and the boasting of what he has and does – comes not from the Father but from the world. The world and its desires pass away, but the man who does the will of God lives forever. (1 John 2:15-17)

Mentally, we have to start packing our bags to leave. Money? Let's use it to build bridges with God's saints, not to line our nests here.

> I tell you, use worldly wealth to gain friends for yourselves, so that when it is gone, you will be welcomed into eternal dwellings. (Luke 16:9)

> There were no needy persons among them. For from time to time those who owned lands or houses sold them, brought the money from

the sales and put it at the apostles' feet, and it was distributed to anyone as he had need. (Acts 4:34-35)

Reputation? It's far better to work on pleasing God, not man.

I care very little if I am judged by you or by any human court; indeed, I do not even judge myself. My conscience is clear, but that does not make me innocent. It is the Lord who judges me. (1 Corinthians 4:3-4)

Our likes and dislikes, our pastimes, our employment, our families, our church life, our possessions, our trials – all have to come under inspection. Are these things taking my heart away from God and his world? Like the weeds in the parable of the sower, so much of this world takes our minds and hearts off our spiritual Mission even after we've professed a conversion. The world has a strong draw on our lives to pull us back from the road to Heaven, and it doesn't seem to matter how far along we may be on that road – we are all susceptible to its pull. As long as we are in this world, we will have to fight this world on our way to the next world.

The church is designed to help you cut the ties to this world and get ready for the next world. All of God's people are on this journey, and it helps tremendously to be among the company of the faithful as they make their pilgrimage to Mt. Zion. They can encourage one another, and "sing the songs of Zion" to put mind and heart "on things above." That is, if the church understands its calling here.

Our goal: perfection

I'm afraid that the unspoken feelings of many a Christian is that "God will take me just as I am!" They're using themselves, as they stand now, as the standard. They feel good (at least they haven't done anything horrible in the recent past), they look good to others, and so they think that they *are* good. Certainly God feels the same away about them. What's to improve when things stand so well?

Little do they know God. Once they get a clear view of the glory of God, they will be horrified to realize that they have done so little to get ready to meet this God. The best of us are going to feel that way. He is a consuming fire; he is infinite; he is power beyond what we dare to imagine; he is holy in a way that we haven't even begun to explore. His world is beyond the comprehension of man's mind. What will this God say about us when we arrive before his throne so ill-prepared to live in this new environment?

> In the year that King Uzziah died, I saw the Lord seated on a throne, high and exalted, and the train of his robe filled the temple … "Woe to me!" I cried. "I am ruined! For I am a man of unclean lips, and I live among a people of unclean lips, and my eyes have seen the King, the LORD Almighty." (Isaiah 6:1,5)

There are many passages of Scripture that teach us to *get ready* for that day. We can't expect to enter Heaven as we are now. For example, in the story of the Ten Virgins, we learn at least three things about those who were allowed into the wedding banquet: they were standing there at the door ready to be let in, they were virgins, and (at least half of them) they had oil in their lamps. Only these were allowed into Heaven. In the story of the unprofitable servant, we learn that only those who have turned the Master's investment to a profit will be allowed into the Kingdom.

In the story of the sheep and the goats, we learn that only those who have been tending to the needs of God's people will be let in. We also have lessons in the Old Testament. In the Temple economy, only those priests who were washed were allowed into God's house. Only those who submitted to David's rule were blessed subjects of the kingdom. Only those with the faith of Abraham were heirs of the covenant.

> Be *perfect*, therefore, as your Heavenly Father is perfect.
> (Matthew 5:48)

So there is a lot to change in us. And the church is the primary place to make this change happen.

The Church – the Family of God

Here are my mother and my brothers. For whoever does the will of my Father in Heaven is my brother and sister and mother. (Matthew 12:49-50)

Let's review a few of the things that we've seen so far. *First*, the church has a **Mission** to accomplish. If our goal is to live with God forever in Heaven, then certain things follow: we have to change from sinners to saints, and we have to cut our ties with this world and get ready to live in God's world. This is going to be a full-time job for both church and church member.

Second, we've seen that we are a part of a Kingdom now, and Christ is the King. We are his subjects. There are positive and negative aspects to this. Positive, that the King will take care of us and do for us those things that are beyond our capabilities. Negative, in that we will learn the hard way, if necessary, that we are no more than servants, and it's not a good idea to rebel against him. The church is not a democracy, thank God. We have a higher hope and glory than what self-rule will take us to.

Third, it ought to be obvious to all except the fool that we have to change a great deal if we want to be a part of this new Kingdom. The ministry of the church is designed to change us: we have to be willing to change, and the changes will be drastic and extensive. None of us are any where near what we need to be. But the resources of the church are specially designed to make that change happen in us.

A Church for Christians – the Family of God

Individuals ... to the core!

But there's another problem that has to be addressed in a church if we want this program to work. Being the modern democratic individuals that we are, we like our freedom – from everyone. Our modern society, in fact, is specially designed to insulate and isolate you from even your next-door neighbor. In past centuries the community was stronger than it is now. People in the same neighborhood, even in the same town, knew each other and related to each other. Now in our modern world, we have isolated ourselves to our insulated living rooms and cut out even the extended family from our pastimes and pursuits.

This same attitude has come into the church. We are a far cry from the original Apostolic church, or even the church down through the centuries in other societies. Christians put up with each other only for an hour or two during Sunday and then return to their safe haven at home. There are many reasons for this, not least the pull of the world and its entertainments and pleasures that compete with the church for our time and attention. But the result is that we know almost nothing about our brothers and sisters at church, nor do we care much about them.

Just to show you that this isn't normal, let's look at a passage from Acts that describes the life of the early church.

> They devoted themselves to the Apostles' teaching and to the fellowship, to the breaking of bread and to prayer. Everyone was filled with awe, and many wonders and miraculous signs were done by the Apostles. All the believers were together and had everything in common. Selling their possessions and goods, they gave to anyone as he had need. Every day they continued to meet together in the temple courts. They broke bread in their homes and ate together with glad and sincere hearts, praising God and enjoying the

favor of all the people. And the Lord added to their number daily those who were being saved. (Acts 2:42-47)

This doesn't describe us. But it does describe many churches around the world in other cultures. The problem is that our modern technological culture has ruined our sense of community, both secular and religious. We are driven by our careers, our 9-to-5 schedules, that make a vital church community virtually impossible. I can't imagine even beginning to address this problem until we dismantle our modern lifestyle that has forced us away from the life of the church.

There's a sinister aspect to our present state of affairs. It's a military maxim that the enemy can defeat us easily if we drift apart from each other. "Divide – and conquer." If we don't assemble together, and pool our resources, and come under one command-and-control structure, and move in unison, we will easily be destroyed. All army commanders understand this principle. It's a shame, however, that so few churches understand this.

In fact, it's not just the army that understands this. People will not hesitate to throw themselves into their jobs, their social clubs, their political causes, with the necessary camaraderie and zeal that it takes to do the job. But for some strange reason they fail to see the need for this unity and zeal in the church. And it's positively disheartening to see them deliberately hurt and destroy the lives of those they profess to love in the church. The church is often a fierce battleground between opposing wills. Pride, lust, politics, greed, and a host of other motives seem to take first priority in church members' hearts instead of the Mission. As a result, we separate from each other, we lose the battle, and many of us don't achieve the Mission.

One thing that a church has to understand and take to heart is that we can't accomplish this Mission on an individual basis. We are not called to be loners. God has made us a Family – because only in unity of spirit and purpose will we achieve our goals.

The Church: the body of Christ

One of the most fundamental changes that happened to us when we became believers is when God made us *one with Christ*. This single idea makes possible our salvation, the righteousness that the Law expects of us, our relationship to God the Father, and our hope of eternal life in Heaven. It's a profound mystery and yet very real and necessary for the believer.

> ... the mystery that has been kept hidden for ages and generations, but is now disclosed to the saints. To them God has chosen to make known among the Gentiles the glorious riches of this mystery, which is Christ in you, the hope of glory. (Colossians 1:26-27)

In fact, all believers make up the entire Body of Christ – again a mystery, but it explains why the same life is in us all.

> Just as each of us has one body with many members, and these members do not all have the same function, so in Christ we who are many form one body, and each member belongs to all the others. (Romans 12:4-5)

Nobody can explain how it happens, but the entire number of Christians down through the ages, and across the world, form one Body that lives by the Spirit of Christ. He is the Head, and we are the "cells," as it were, and parts of the Body that make a whole. None of us is unnecessary to the body, and every one of us is needed for its function and well-being.

The idea is that we live *together*; if we pull away, we die, just as a part of your physical body will die if it's cut off from the rest. We need what the rest of the body provides for us, and they need us.

We already saw the role of spiritual gifts in the church. Each part of the body is gifted for the benefit of the whole body; we each rely on one another for what we ourselves can't do. This is the way that the Lord changes us all – being in close proximity to the power and wisdom of Heaven, through our brothers and sisters, strengthens and guides us all.

The Church – the family of God

The image of the church being the Body of Christ is useful to teach us some vital principles of the life and function of the church. But it's not the only image we can use. The Bible also calls us the **family** of God in order to teach us about other principles of church life.

The passage in Matthew that we referenced above shows us what Jesus thinks of the family of God – it was more important to him than his earthly family.

> While Jesus was still talking to the crowd, his mother and brothers stood outside, wanting to speak to him. Someone told him, "Your mother and brothers are standing outside, wanting to speak to you." He replied to him, "Who is my mother, and who are my brothers?" Pointing to his disciples, he said, "Here are my mother and my brothers. For whoever does the will of my Father in Heaven is my brother and sister and mother." (Matthew 12:49-50)

The reason he feels this way is because he's putting together a new family, one that will outlast the destruction of this world and live on in Heaven. Earthly families don't often stick together on spiritual matters. The church, however, is made up of people who are vitally concerned with the state of their souls and how to go to Heaven. They are there to work on *this* project. And since Jesus was primarily in this world for that one reason, he of course focuses his attention, affection and work on those saints who want to go.

> Both the one who makes men holy and those who are made holy are of the same family. So Jesus is not ashamed to call them brothers. He says, "I will declare your name to my brothers; in the presence of the congregation I will sing your praises." And again, "I will put my trust in him." And again he says, "Here am I, and the children God has given me." Since the children have flesh and blood, he too shared in their humanity so that by his death he might destroy him who holds the power of death – that is, the devil – and free those who all their lives were held in slavery by their fear of death. (Hebrews 2:11-15)

Like it or not, Jesus has little time for anybody else. "I was sent only to the lost sheep of Israel." (Matthew 15:24) He loves his brothers and sisters; he works day and night for their benefit; he has poured out his life for them. They are his family – children born of his Spirit by the will of God.

> Yet to all who received him, to those who believed in his name, he gave the right to become children of God – children born not of natural descent, nor of human decision or a husband's will, but born of God. (John 1:12-13)

Are these Christians so much different from the rest of humanity that they warrant his complete attention and love? They are more different than you can know! They are members of a new race of man. Whereas our present world is populated with children of Adam – and rebellious and cursed as a result of that ancestry – the people of God have been created along new lines. They are designed to know and love and serve the spiritual God *without fail*, forever.

> So it is written: "The first man Adam became a living being"; the last Adam, a life-giving spirit. The spiritual did not come first, but the natural, and after that the spiritual. The first man was of the dust of the earth, the second man from Heaven. As was the earthly man, so are those who are of the earth; and as is the man from Heaven, so also are those who are of Heaven. And just as we have borne the likeness of the earthly man, so shall we bear the likeness of the man from Heaven. (1 Corinthians 15:45-49)

We can see this "new man" in Jesus himself, who was the pioneer, the forerunner, of the new race. But we also see this "new man" in the life of the church, as the Spirit of Christ conforms us into Christ's image. As the Spirit works among the church members, life pours out among them and re-creates each of them into the "new man."

> His purpose was to create in himself one new man out of the two, thus making peace, and in this one body to reconcile both of them to God through the cross, by which he put to death their hostility. He came and preached peace to you who were far away and peace to those who were near. For through him we both have access to the Father by one Spirit. Consequently, you are no longer foreigners and aliens, but fellow citizens with God's people and members of God's household. (Ephesians 2:15-19)

Abraham's children

This idea of the family of God goes way back to the beginning of the Bible. In Genesis 1-11 we learn what God created the world to be, and what man (and Satan as his partner-in-crime!) turned God's perfect world into. Then in Genesis 12 we are introduced to one of the most important characters of the Bible – Abraham.

God chose Abraham out of all the peoples of the earth and gave him a precious gift, the Covenant. We don't have time to get into the specifics here, but the Covenant was nothing less than the Gospel of Christ. Paul tells us this:

> The Scripture foresaw that God would justify the Gentiles by faith, and announced the Gospel in advance to Abraham: "All nations will be blessed through you." (Galatians 3:8)

In fact, Paul also tells us that any of us who have the hope of salvation in Christ and eternal life in Heaven is actually an heir of this Covenant made with Abraham.

> If you belong to Christ, then you are Abraham's seed, and heirs according to the promise. (Galatians 329)

Jesus showed us a remarkable scene unfolding in Heaven, as Abraham's spiritual children start gathering around his feet for the final wedding feast.

> There will be weeping there, and gnashing of teeth, when you see Abraham, Isaac and Jacob and all the prophets in the kingdom of God, but you yourselves thrown out. People will come from east and west and

north and south, and will take their places at the feast in the kingdom of God. (Luke 13:28-29)

As Jesus points out here, it takes more than a physical descent from Abraham to be considered an heir of his Covenant. We need the *faith* of Abraham to be able to claim salvation. Unbelieving Jews are not getting in! But believing Gentiles will be welcomed in as part of the family – they have the family characteristics.

God's new family

This story also brings up another important point. The Jews think that they are automatically deserving of Heaven since they are physically descended from Abraham; they are mistaken about this. But so are a lot of people in church mistaken about the idea of "family." We have to distinguish between earthly families and God's spiritual family. God doesn't draw the line in the same places that we want to see them. The Jews erred in considering genetic descent as a qualification; so do modern Christians, it seems.

Jesus knew that many people would make the mistake of putting their earthly families above the church. He spoke to this issue on many occasions. For example, here is what he expects from earthly families.

> For I have come to turn 'a man against his father, a daughter against her mother, a daughter-in-law against her mother-in-law – a man's enemies will be the members of his own household.' (Matthew 10:35-36)

As far as he was concerned, he sees that we will encounter the most problems with our own families. As we struggle to make our way toward Heaven, our families will often turn out to be our most bitter enemies. Jesus was pretty skeptical about how useful our families are going to be on our spiritual journey. In fact, there are about ten places in the Gospels where Jesus talks about our families, and none of them are positive – he was either indifferent about the subject, or downright skeptical. He sees no help from that quarter.

He also knows our hearts. When it comes time to choose between family and church, we will almost always choose the family. That's a mistake. Our earthly families will rarely follow us to Heaven; the church family, however, is going to be there waiting for us. How willing are we to follow our brothers and sisters in the faith when our families demand that we turn aside and spend our energies on them alone? What will we do when our families demand that we adhere to their values, when Heaven calls from a different direction? There will be many faced with that dilemma, and Jesus takes a dim view of those who turn away from the church for the sake of their families.

> Anyone who loves his father or mother more than me is not worthy of me; anyone who loves his son or daughter more than me is not worthy of me; and anyone who does not take his cross and follow me is not worthy of me. (Matthew 10:37-38)

It's not that Jesus thinks ill of our families; it's just that he knows that, for the most part, they won't share your new spiritual values. As much as you want them to join you in church life, they rarely will. Most families will divide over this issue of Christianity – you've no doubt seen it already and know that it's true. It's sad, and it ought not to be, but it's a fact. Those churches nowadays that try to build a "family-oriented ministry" didn't get their ideas, nor their optimism that such a thing will work, from Jesus.

So the Lord refuses to draw the line of God's family around our earthly families. The church is our new family now, and like John Bunyan's Pilgrim, you must go with the church even if your family won't follow you. Here in the church you will find like-minded pilgrims on their way to Heaven. They will care about your spiritual life and are willing to help you on your journey. They have the resources and the calling to help you. They care about your soul in a way that no other earthly institution does.

Your brothers and sisters in church share your spiritual characteristics. They have the same faith that you have, the same Spirit, the same hope of Heaven, they deal with the same spiritual treasures that you value, they have seen the same spiritual Kingdom that you have seen, they are growing the same spiritual fruit in their lives that you are growing. You have much more in common with these people than even your physical family. You are all being groomed and prepared for a new life in Heaven, whereas this world, with all its associations and relationships, is doomed to be destroyed.

In fact, you can run across a believer in any part of the world and discover this mystical unity of purpose and life. You may be citizens of different countries, and disagree violently on political or cultural issues. But if you are both Christians, you walk on a higher plane than the petty differences of this world. You are both destined to live with God. You will find many things in common that show the hand of Christ forming and preparing you for God's world. So, we can't predict how or where God will draw that line that separates his family from the rest of the world, but we will know it when we meet someone inside that line – they will be part of the church. We won't find such kindred spirits in any other earthly relationship.

Working together

Now that we've explored the principle of the family of God, we need to examine what that will look like on the church level. What does it mean that a Christian is a part of the family of God?

Let me say first that a church will never work unless both the leadership and the membership are agreed, and determined, about this point. *We are brothers and sisters.* We are not individuals who can live without each other. God put us together in profound wisdom; he made it possible for us to achieve our Mission as a family, not by ourselves.

And of course it's also true that we can't separate from each other over any little problem or whim. Just as physical family members can't deny their relationship, despite problems, so the members of God's household can't deny their relationships. In other words, if you refuse to work out problems and leave the church "offended" with someone, you are only postponing the issue, not solving it. God is going to force you to come back to this problem and deal with it sometime, somewhere. The secret is that it's easier to take care of this the first time around, not the second. Leaving your brothers over some trivial issue only causes even more hurt and suffering that has to be addressed. Then you will have that new crime to answer for as well as the original problem.

The spiritual skill that makes the family work is love. That's why the subject of love is so prevalent in the Bible.

> My command is this: Love each other as I have loved you. Greater love has no one than this, that he lay down his life for his friends. (John 15:12-13)

Here is the command *and* the definition. We must love each other as Jesus loves us. Spend some time on that idea for a while! And to head off any wrong notions on what "love" might mean, Jesus tells us: we must give until it hurts; we must make sure our brother has what he needs, even if it means we have to go without; we must put ourselves out of the picture so that our brother can get into it; we must "consider others better than ourselves." (Philippians 2:3) We must put aside our pride and

A Church for Christians – the Family of God

bear with our brother's immaturity. We must spend time and energy for our brother's benefit.

Now most people in church today don't love like this. How do I know? Simply because we don't even know our brother and his circumstances! How can we *love* him if we're not even close enough to him to know what he needs? And how can we *love* him if we are so ready to declare war against him over trivial matters?

> This is how we know who the children of God are and who the children of the devil are: Anyone who does not do what is right is not a child of God; nor is anyone who does not love his brother. (1 John 3:10)

> If anyone has material possessions and sees his brother in need but has no pity on him, how can the love of God be in him? (1 John 3:17)

> If anyone says, "I love God," yet hates his brother, he is a **liar**. For anyone who does not love his brother, whom he has seen, cannot love God, whom he has not seen. And he has given us this command: Whoever loves God must also love his brother. (1 John 4:20-21)

John obviously feels very strongly about this matter. He has seen a lot of people claim to love their brother and yet their claim was empty. When power or money come to the table, we find out who really loves who! As far as he is concerned, there are a lot of fake "Christians" in today's church who don't love anybody but themselves. They are lying about their "faith."

We might object to such strong language, but John presses his point home and makes it simple for us to understand: they are a **L…I…A…R**. People who are only out for themselves, who willingly hurt the sheep to get ahead, who despise authority –

such people, as Jude tells us, are a blemish on the church and should not be tolerated any more than they would tolerate Satan himself among them.

> These men are blemishes at your love feasts, eating with you without the slightest qualm – shepherds who feed only themselves. They are clouds without rain, blown along by the wind; autumn trees, without fruit and uprooted – twice dead. They are wild waves of the sea, foaming up their shame; wandering stars, for whom blackest darkness has been reserved forever. Enoch, the seventh from Adam, prophesied about these men: "See, the Lord is coming with thousands upon thousands of his holy ones to judge everyone, and to convict all the ungodly of all the ungodly acts they have done in the ungodly way, and of all the harsh words ungodly sinners have spoken against him." These men are grumblers and faultfinders; they follow their own evil desires; they boast about themselves and flatter others for their own advantage. (Jude 12-16)

The church can't work if it's filled with a lot of self-seeking, self-serving, proud, rebellious troublemakers who will stop at nothing (including hurting others) to get what they want.

But your church can survive, even with all sorts of problems, as long as everyone genuinely loves each other.

> Above all, love each other deeply, because love covers over a multitude of sins. Offer hospitality to one another without grumbling. Each one should use whatever gift he has received to serve others, faithfully administering God's grace in its various forms. (1 Peter 4:8-10)

That love will get to work to *solve* the problems, not generate new ones. That love will bring everyone along in the Mission, and not leave anybody behind. That love will put others first, and not compete against them. As you can see, the gift of love helps each person achieve his goal – because he has so many people at hand who are willing and able to help him get there.

How does it work? Well, we can again use the early church as an example. We've already seen that their church did these things:

- They devoted themselves to:
    - the Apostles' teaching,
    - to fellowship,
    - to breaking bread together,
    - to prayer.
- They spent time together.
- They had everything in common.
- They sold their possessions and gave the proceeds to their needy.
- They met every day in the Temple courts.
- They met in their homes and ate together.

In other words, they were free with what they owned, and they liked being around each other – a lot. We are also told, in Acts 4, that there were no needy persons among them.

A holy priesthood

Another aspect of the church that makes it work is that everyone is doing their job – for the sake of others. Jesus has given us spiritual resources to help the church achieve its Mission.

They are called the spiritual gifts of the church, and they are given by the Spirit himself. These gifts can be found listed in these passages: Romans 12:6-8; 1 Corinthians 12:8-10; Ephesians 4:11; and 1 Peter 4:10-11. Furthermore, though we often call any ability a "gift" even in the church, only the ones that the Word specifies as a gift qualifies.

A spiritual gift is a God-given ability to help others see Christ more clearly and draw closer to him in faith. And that is precisely what is needed. Christ is our life; he's our salvation; he is the wisdom and power of God. Drawing close to him is achieving our goal of living with God in sinless perfection. So if someone else can help me do that – well, that's where the gifts come in.

The Old Testament teaches us about the functions and roles of the priests in Israel. They provided a critical role in the life of God's people. Interestingly, in the New Testament we learn that we *all* have become priests in God's house.

> You also, like living stones, are being built into a spiritual house to be a holy priesthood, offering spiritual sacrifices acceptable to God through Jesus Christ. (1 Peter 2:5)
>
> But you are a chosen people, a royal priesthood, a holy nation, a people belonging to God, that you may declare the praises of him who called you out of darkness into his wonderful light. (1 Peter 2:9)
>
> To him who loves us and has freed us from our sins by his blood, and has made us to be a kingdom and priests to serve his God and Father – to him be glory and power for ever and ever! (Revelation 1:5-6)

This means, then, that we now have an obligation to minister to others, just as the Old Testament priests did. We are in the position of bringing the blessing of the presence and treasures of God to our brothers and sisters in need. The result of this faithful work among us, on the part of us all, is the living Temple where God intends to live forever.

> In him the whole building is joined together and rises to become a holy Temple in the Lord. And in him you too are being built together to become a dwelling in which God lives by his Spirit. (Ephesians 2:21-22)

A change of heart

I hope you realize that, in order to be of such help to each other, our natures have to change. This too is an area where we are sadly lacking in today's churches. Even in conservative churches, new members are welcomed with open arms – but then their growth comes to a complete stop. Everyone assumes two things: first, that they don't need much more than what they received at conversion to be good Christians. And second, anything that they manage to get in addition to that, they will have to get it on their own. There's certainly no training or rigorous program in place to get them to maturity.

The result is that we still have a lot of nasty character traits about us that too often show themselves in difficult church circumstances. The sins of the flesh are simmering below the surface and nobody is working on them, or even admitting their presence.

> The acts of the sinful nature are obvious: sexual immorality, impurity and debauchery; idolatry and witchcraft; hatred, discord, jealousy, fits of rage, selfish ambition, dissensions, factions and envy; drunkenness, orgies, and the like. I warn you, as I did before, that those who live like this will not inherit the kingdom of God. (Galatians 5:19-21)

Probably every church has its horror stories of church splits, arguments and fights, hostile board meetings, simmering feuds. And that's just one aspect of the sinful flesh. There is adultery and immorality going on in churches, greed and corruption, lying and deceiving, politicking, apathy and laziness – this sordid list describes the church as well as the world. When things like these come up, everyone wonders how it could happen in a *church!* The fact is that nobody addressed this spiritual reality – neither the pulpit nor the pew. Everyone ignored it, thinking that if nobody talked about it, then maybe it all went away when they got converted. It didn't go away, and it never will, as long as people don't directly confront the enemy and systematically *destroy* it before it destroys them.

In order to even get along with each other, let alone do something good for one another, we have to crucify this junk in our hearts and replace it with the fruit of the Spirit.

> But the fruit of the Spirit is love, joy, peace, patience, kindness, goodness, faithfulness, gentleness and self-control. Against such things there is no law. Those who belong to Christ Jesus have crucified the sinful nature with its passions and desires. (Galatians 5:22-24)

Someone who lives like this is a *nice person*. They will be a great source of help toward others. You aren't going to have any problems out of them. Fill a church with people like this, and you have a church with a Mission! Everyone will be busy ministering to the needs of others.

Heaven on earth

People have often wished that life could be a utopia – a perfect world. And many thinkers have come up with schemes to create that kind of a world. But they are all doomed to fail, because man can't make such a world come about.

But Christ can – and will. The world he is creating is not only going to be perfect, but it's going to last forever in its perfection. In fact, the church is the foretaste of that perfect world that is coming. *It is the only place on earth where such things can happen.* The most strict government on earth can only pass laws and hope to terrify people into submission. The Lord, however, puts his Spirit in the hearts of his people and changes them from the inside out. He makes them *want* to be righteous and holy.

The church alone has the resources to make this happen. Notice in the following passage that Paul assumes that they will be like Christ *if* they have certain spiritual realities in place.

> If you have any encouragement from being united with Christ, if any comfort from his love, if any fellowship with the Spirit, if any tenderness and compassion, then make my joy complete by being like-minded, having the same love, being one in spirit and purpose. Do nothing out of selfish ambition or vain conceit, but in humility consider others better than yourselves. Each of you should look not only to your own interests, but also to the interests of others. Your attitude should be the same as that of Christ Jesus. (Philippians 2:1-5)

The church that you are in could be laboring under all sorts of difficulties; but if the members are truly united with Christ and have his Spirit in them, there is hope. They will see each other as family, and they will put themselves out for the benefit of each other. To them, the church is their life. As the Psalmist said, "God sets the lonely in families." (Psalm 68:6) The church is a garden where our fruit will grow. The church is a household, where the family can grow and mature. But in order to succeed,

A Church for Christians – the Family of God

the church has to be bound together as a family and care for each other.

If this doesn't happen in the church, it's certainly not going to happen anywhere else. Because the world doesn't care at all about you. In the world, people gravitate toward the young, the strong, the rich, and the beautiful. But in the church, we are to gravitate toward the lowly, the forsaken, the despised of the world – those in need. Our family are those who are "hungering and thirsting after righteousness." We Christians are the only ones who will care about them, because we know what it's like for someone to love us.

> But God demonstrates his own love for us in this: While we were still sinners, Christ died for us. (Romans 5:8)

The Church – live by the Spirit

So I say, live by the Spirit, and you will not gratify the desires of the sinful nature. (Galatians 5:16)

If it were up to us, the church would never work. Our age is infected with the spirit of lawlessness. We get along with each other for a while, but something will come up – a question of authority, money, pride – and soon we start fighting with each other.

Even if we agree that the church is a Kingdom, and that only Jesus is King, we have little idea of what that means on a practical level. Before long we either want to run things our own way, or we refuse to submit to the leadership. Oftentimes leading a church is like trying to herd cats – they all want to go their own way, and they fuss and scratch and fight when you try to steer them the right way!

The problem is that you can't *make* people want to do the right thing. The human heart is beyond the reach of man's laws. Even the best of governments can't change us into God's image. Even if everyone promised that they would behave themselves, somewhere down the road they're going to break that promise. For example, when David took the throne and became king over Israel, all the people promised him that they would behave. Not only did they show their colors when they repeatedly rebelled against him, within a generation of his death the tribes of the North completely rebelled and formed their own nation, in spite of their promises to him and to God.

So, how do you get people to cooperate and work together? If the Kingdom of Heaven is eternal, and must not be subject to the whims of man, how are we going to motivate people to persevere and do things God's way? More laws won't help, since people will quickly break the laws when it suits them. Candy doesn't help either, though many churches try this. They think that if they offer people sweet things then they can draw them in and keep their interest. The problem is that people get tired of your sweets after a while, and they'll leave and go after bigger prizes down the street.

The answer, of course, is that God has to change their hearts. He does this by his Spirit, who is a power beyond what this world can comprehend. When you have a Christian filled with the Spirit of Christ, now you have someone who will obey God willingly, from the heart, and the church has a real chance to work. The Spirit is the only motivator that works in the church.

Misunderstandings

Before we look at how the Spirit drives a successful church, we need first to correct some wrong notions that people have about the Spirit.

The Holy Spirit is key to the life of the church, as well as to the Christian. When Jesus was resurrected, he promised his disciples that he would give them his Spirit – because he was going to a place that they couldn't follow.

> And I will ask the Father, and he will give you another Counselor to be with you forever – the Spirit of truth. The world cannot accept him, because it neither sees him nor knows him. But you know him, for he lives with you and will be in you. I will not leave you as orphans; I will come to you. (John 14:16-18)

The Spirit of Christ is the very life of Christ; the Spirit embodies the righteousness of Christ, his power and wisdom, the openness to God, his Son-ship, his eternity. If someone has the Spirit of Christ in them, he literally lives the life of Jesus himself; or, put another way, Jesus lives in him.

> I have been crucified with Christ and I no longer live, but Christ lives in me. The life I live in the body, I live by faith in the Son of God, who loved me and gave himself for me. (Galatians 2:20)

This reality assures us of a place in Heaven with God. It means that all sorts of good things will happen to us – the very things that have happened to Jesus. The Spirit does something that the Law can never do.

> Through Christ Jesus the law of the Spirit of life set me free from the law of sin and death. (Romans 8:2)

So it's amazing to me how certain errors have crept into the church about the work of the Spirit. Obviously many people don't understand what the Spirit has come to do for us.

- ***Some believe that the Spirit is only for Charismatics.*** The Pentecostals and Charismatics focus on the Spirit almost to the exclusion of everything else. As a result, they read the entire Bible in the light of spiritual experiences that they crave, as if Christianity were simply a matter of jumping from one spiritual high to another. The purpose of the Spirit, to them, is to give them a vision or a word from Heaven or some other spiritual ecstasy, like some of the prophets of the Old Testament. Their excesses are well known.

  The problem is that the more conservative Christian groups tend to pull away from any discussion on the Spirit because of those excesses. They don't want to be branded as Charismatics or spiritual fanatics. I've heard seminary professors admit that their denomination doesn't have much to teach about the Spirit of God from fear that they might be looked at as Pentecostals.

This is a terrible road to take. Just because one group goes to excess on the subject doesn't mean that the rest of us ought to ignore it. There is a *Biblical* explanation of the work of the Spirit, and we are obligated to find it and follow it. If we steer away from the subject out of fear of the Charismatics, we will miss out on the life that Jesus has for us – and our churches will never work.

- ***Some believe that we get the Spirit some time after our conversion.*** The way they read certain passages in the Bible, they think that conversion comes first and then we get "filled" with the Spirit during a "second blessing" – if and when it happens.

This can't be true. When a person becomes a Christian, his name is written in the Book of Life (Revelation 21:27) and he's on the way to Heaven. The problem is that nobody can get to Heaven without the Spirit! That's his role for the church. If someone claimed to be a Christian and yet didn't have the Spirit in him, it would be like saying that a baby was born dead.

There are spiritual realities that happen when a person is converted, things that can't happen without the Spirit. He sees God; he has faith in Jesus as his Savior; he repents of his sin and turns to holiness. He's living in a spiritual world now – at least his soul is, even if his body is still drawn to this world. A war has begun between the two halves of his nature: an awakened soul, and the troublesome flesh. That war shows the presence of the Spirit in his life.

> For the sinful nature desires what is contrary to the Spirit, and the Spirit what is contrary to the sinful nature. They are in conflict with each other, so that you do not do what you want. (Galatians 5:17)

No, when we get converted, the Spirit comes into our souls for good, to live there and direct us to Heaven. That's the mark of a true Christian.

> Having believed, you were marked in him with a seal, the promised Holy Spirit, who is a deposit guaranteeing our inheritance until the redemption of those who are God's possession – to the praise of his glory. (Ephesians 1:13-14)

The functions of the Spirit

Leaving aside the ecstasies of the Charismatics, the Spirit does two things for the ordinary Christian. These two things are fundamental to his spiritual walk in this world. Some people are craving visions and tongues, but the child of God has more important matters to attend to. You can, like King Saul, be like "one of the prophets" (1 Samuel 10:12), and yet lose your soul.

- ***First, the Spirit reveals to us the world of God.*** Until we became Christians, we had no idea of what God was like, nor of the world that he lives in. We thought that the only reality was this physical world that we were born into. Then, when we saw Jesus, the Spirit pulled away the curtains of this world and let us see the truth about Christ. We saw his spiritual side, and the spiritual benefits of closing with him. We saw spiritual treasures there that far outweigh the empty treasures of this world.

The Spirit *reveals* the things of God to us.

> However, as it is written: "No eye has seen, no ear has heard, no mind has conceived what God has prepared for those who love him" – but God has revealed it to us by his Spirit. (1 Corinthians 2:9-10)

That revelation is vital for our Christian walk. We see the true worth of Christ. We see our spiritual poverty without him. We see the urgent need to take hold of him, to stand on him like on a rock, while the world around us falls apart. We see why Heaven is better than this world. Before we saw all of this, we were content enough with this physical world of ours; but after the revelation we feel like "aliens and strangers" in this world and are longing for the next one.

I hope you can understand why this work of the Spirit is so vital to the life of the church. The church constantly deals in the spiritual currency of Heaven. It holds out the Word of Life as our hope, and warns us away from this world. The ministry of the church leads the sheep to the Shepherd, to the Master and King, to submit to his rule over them and enjoy his spiritual blessings. The church addresses the one fatal problem of mankind, the one obstacle between us and our hope – our sin – and calls on us to see how urgent this matter is of crucifying and destroying what is between us and our God.

Before we go astray here, let's establish exactly how – or *where* – the Spirit is going to reveal all of this to us: through the ***Word***. Only in the Bible will we see God and his world. The Bible alone is truth. The Spirit and the Word always work together to reveal the truth to God's people.

> Yet a time is coming and has now come when the true worshipers will worship the Father in spirit and truth, for they are the kind of worshipers the Father seeks. God is spirit, and his worshipers must worship in ***spirit*** and in ***truth***. (John 4:23-24)

This too fits right in with the church's ministry. Much of its work is focused on preaching and teaching; the job of the pastors and teachers is to bring God's truth to the people, and help them deal with it. And if the members have the Spirit of Christ in them, they will listen to God's Word, believe it, and live by it.

If the Spirit isn't present in a person's heart, the unique spiritual ministry of the church is wasted on him. He will want entertainment, church bazaars, picnics and parties, social contacts, "celebrations" – but he won't be the least interested in the benefit of its ministry to his soul. On the other hand, a spiritual Christian comes to church for what only the church can give him – that vital contact with God and his world. The two fit together.

- ***Second, the Spirit empowers us to live in that spiritual world.*** If we only saw our hope from a distance, it would be blessing enough. But God goes one step further and gives us a taste of that Promised

Land, like he did for the Israelites with the grapes of Eshcol. (Numbers 13:24)

> But you will receive power when the Holy Spirit comes on you; and you will be my witnesses in Jerusalem, and in all Judea and Samaria, and to the ends of the earth. (Acts 1:8)

We weren't born with the ability to know God, let alone take advantage of a spiritual world. Who among us would know the way to Heaven? How would we get there? We are stuck in this world, like helpless criminals in prison, until the Spirit frees us from the shackles of the physical and sets our feet in high places.

Primarily we taste these spiritual realities when we pray – which is why Paul stressed the importance of praying in the Spirit.

> And pray in the Spirit on all occasions with all kinds of prayers and requests. (Ephesians 6:18)

When the Spirit helps us, we not only see God in his glory but we can touch him and serve him. We find new strength, purpose, and wisdom in him. Our physical lives become service to a spiritual God. We please him with our walk of faith. We become holy, set aside for his purposes. Our cups of cold water help to build his Kingdom on earth. We can resist the Enemy in his Name and power. We serve our brothers and sisters in the faith with the power and wisdom that Christ gives us in his Spirit. We find that we now have all sorts of new skills – spiritual skills – to help build this spiritual Temple that we are going to live in forever.

> ... to prepare God's people for works of service, so that the body of Christ may be built up until we all reach unity in the faith and in the knowledge of the Son of God and become mature, attaining to the whole measure of the fullness of Christ. (Ephesians 4:12-13)

These spiritual gifts are critical for the life of the church. The pastor is not the only one doing the work! We all are priests, serving God in his Temple, and able to bring God's blessings to his people. The Christian who not only understands this, but is in touch with the world of God in a vital way, is ready and able to put his back into the work of the church – which is the only way it will work.

Follow his leading

The church is God's spiritual work on earth; in that it is unique. Not only does God bring a power from another world to bear on this world's problems, but the solution consists of leading us through this world to that next world. The point of Christianity is not to stay here, nor is it to make our life here more comfortable. The point is to get to the Promised Land. Remember our goal? It's to live with God forever, in Heaven – not here.

So if God gives us his Spirit to make this happen, it makes sense that we must *follow* the Spirit as he leads us out of this world and into the next. That's why Paul told us to follow the leading of the Spirit.

> Since we live by the Spirit, let us keep in step with the Spirit. (Galatians 5:25)

This doesn't mean, as some would believe, that we should end up in desert places or high mountains, as if there are spiritual "resorts" in this world where we can better commune with God. As Jesus told us in John 4, there are no such special places in this world. The road that we use to get to Heaven is a spiritual road. In short, Jesus is the way to Heaven.

First, to remind you again of the vital necessity of the *Bible*, the Word of God is the way of life. The Spirit will lead you back to the Bible again and again to get you ready for life with God; it can't be done in any other way. If your Christianity is missing the daily and active work of the Bible on your soul, you aren't in the way of life. The Bible is more important to your spiritual life than food is for your body.

> Man does not live on bread alone, but on every word that comes from the mouth of God. (Matthew 4:4)

Second, remember too that the Spirit is leading you to *Heaven* – not to anything in this world. The mystics might be led to do strange things and go to strange places – and they consider themselves more holy for having done so – but we ordinary mortals have a higher calling. Eventually we will be living with God, in Heaven, and that goal is far beyond our present reach.

> Since, then, you have been raised with Christ, set your hearts on things above, where Christ is seated at the right hand of God. Set your minds on things above, not on earthly things. (Colossians 3:1-2)

There are some essential things that we have to do to get ready for that high calling – things common to all of God's children.

The Spirit is going to get you started on those things. *Follow him.* He knows what you need, and he knows what he's doing. If you need some sins and rebellious ways pruned out of your life, submit yourself to his discipline as he puts you through the trials necessary for that pruning. If you need some of the graces of Christ in your dealings with other people, submit to the Spirit as he trains you, in his own unique ways, to bear that fruit in your relationships with others. In all these things the Spirit is faithfully preparing you to be holy, and righteous, in all your dealings with God and man. Only then will you be fit to live with God.

You will find that much of his leading will consist of crucifying the flesh. This problem of our old nature is more serious than you might imagine. Too many people think that, after they are converted, it will be smooth sailing from there. They go to church without the least notion that they have much more work to do on their hearts. True, Jesus covers them with his righteousness. But underneath that legal protection is still a wicked heart.

> The heart is deceitful above all things and beyond cure. Who can understand it? (Jeremiah 17:9)

The Spirit understands it, however, and he won't let you just sit back and not work on it. Something will come up that will successfully uncover what you really are – to yourself and to others. Then you will see, when it's too late to save your pride, that you aren't the perfect person that you thought you were! And if you resist the leading of the Spirit to change your heart, he will keep bringing it to the forefront until, crippled and suffering under the weight of your sin and its consequences, you finally give up and agree to change to his standards.

> For if you live according to the sinful nature, you will die; but if by the Spirit you put to death the misdeeds of the body, you will live. (Romans 8:130

The goal is nothing short of perfection. The Spirit's job is to make us look like Christ – to have his image in us, as well as his legal righteousness.

> Now the Lord is the Spirit, and where the Spirit of the Lord is, there is freedom. And we, who with unveiled faces all reflect the Lord's glory, are being transformed into his likeness with ever-increasing glory, which comes from the Lord, who is the Spirit. (2 Corinthians 3:17-18)

And in case we agree with this in principle but still prove to be proud and rebellious when it comes to the details, the Bible tells us what our lives should look like in the end.

> But the fruit of the Spirit is love, joy, peace, patience, kindness, goodness, faithfulness, gentleness and self-control. Against such things there is no law. Those who belong to Christ Jesus have crucified the sinful nature with its passions and desires. (Galatians 5:22-24)

So you see, Christianity isn't a matter of strutting around in our Christian pride and showing off how much we know. It's a *humbling* experience. We have to change our sinful hearts to the goal of Christ's perfect heart. Remember, the church is a spiritual hospital – we are there to get cured, not to show off. Jesus, as he told us, didn't come to save the "righteous" but to save *sinners*.

If people in the church are working on these spiritual issues, and their lives show their progress in these areas, then the church is accomplishing its Mission. But if people don't come to church for this reason, the church will never work. Everyone has to agree that the church will only work if the members are led by the Spirit to do what the Spirit has for us – our salvation from sin. In other words, they are going to be truly converted. Only true Christians are going to work on the Mission.

New spiritual skills

We've seen what the Spirit will do in our lives – he *reveals* the world of God to us, and *empowers* us to take advantage of what we see. But he also has to put corresponding skills inside our hearts to make sure all of this happens. We aren't capable of handling what the Spirit has for us unless we acquire special spiritual skills.

This is important to understand. These skills that God gives us are *gifts*, not something that we have to develop on our own. We can't do this on our own. We are entering a new world here, with realities that are beyond our comprehension, let alone beyond our powers to grasp. If God wishes us to participate in his glory, he simply has to give us (I mean that in a practical sense – he doesn't *have* to give us anything!) the things we need to survive in Heaven.

You will find these three gifts listed in a number of places in the Bible. For example, here are all three mentioned in one passage.

> We continually remember before our God and Father your work produced by **faith**, your labor prompted by **love**, and your endurance inspired by **hope** in our Lord Jesus Christ. (1 Thessalonians 1:3)

Faith, hope and love are the spiritual edge that we need to escape the common fate of humanity and enter Heaven. With them, we can take advantage of the special spiritual ministry of the church and prepare for life with God. Without them, the church's ministry will be wasted on us.

- **Faith** – *the ability to see God's spiritual world.* When the Spirit "turns the lights on" in our hearts, he gives us the corresponding ability to see – and take advantage of – the world that he's showing us. This is faith.

   > I am the light of the world. Whoever follows me will never walk in darkness, but will have the light of life. (John 8:12)

   When the author of Hebrews defines faith as "being sure of what we hope for and certain of what we do not see" (Hebrews 11:1) he is referring to this spiritual insight that goes beyond our physical world. We *know* now that God is there; we *know* what he's like because we've seen him in his Word. This isn't something that we trained ourselves to be able to do; it happens naturally for the child of God. It's a gift put into his heart to enable him to know God.

   > For it is by grace you have been saved, through faith – and this not from yourselves, it is the gift of God – not by works, so that no one can boast. (Ephesians 2:8)

   Without faith, the preaching and teaching of the Word in church will be wasted on you, like the seed sown on the path. (Matthew 13:19) The preacher is pointing out spiritual truths to you, aspects of God's world that it is essential for you to understand. But only a corresponding faith on your part will bring fruit to the transaction. It won't be wasted on you; it will bear the appropriate fruit in your heart and life that the Spirit intended for it.

> So is my Word that goes out from my mouth: It will not return to me empty, but will accomplish what I desire and achieve the purpose for which I sent it. (Isaiah 55:11)

- **Hope** – *our desire for God's world.* Hope is not what many people think it is. It's not *wishing* that something *might* happen. It's based on a certainty that it *will* happen. Because of faith, we know that God's promises are sure and certain. Who can doubt what they've seen?

Hope adds *longing* for those things to our hearts. We want what we see; we will not be satisfied with this world, and our desire is for God and his world. Our hearts are on God and his world now, not on this world.

> Whom have I in Heaven but you? And earth has nothing I desire besides you. (Psalm 73:25)

Abraham, when the Lord called him to pick up his possessions and family and move to Canaan, actually went! Can you imagine an old man in his eighties doing such a drastic thing? Yet something in what God showed him about this new life was appealing to him, so much so that he willingly put his old life behind him and embraced the new life with God.

As Christians we've been called to a new world. Most people ignore this call – they don't see anything about God or Heaven worth looking into. But that's exactly the point with the true Christian: he has seen it (from afar) and he *wants* it. He puts his heart on "things above" now.

> I pray also that the eyes of your heart may be enlightened in order that you may know the hope to which he has called you, the riches of his glorious inheritance in the saints, and his incomparably great power for us who believe. (Ephesians 1:18-19)

> Since, then, you have been raised with Christ, set your hearts on things above, where Christ is seated at the right hand of God. Set your minds on things above, not on earthly things. (Colossians 3:1-2)

It's a difficult thing for leaders in the church to keep people's interest in spiritual matters. In fact, in our day the church has resorted to all sorts of tricks – what I call "candy" – to keep people coming back. That will never make a church work. What works is when people actually "hunger and thirst for righteousness." (Matthew 5:6) You don't need candy for people who have a hope for Heaven. The Spirit makes them excited to learn about God, anxious to please him, determined to build his Kingdom. A church that ministers to Christians who have put their hearts "on things above" will work.

- **<u>Love</u>** – ***the willingness to leave all behind for God and the church.*** There are three words for "love" in the Greek language. The first is the physical love between man and woman – "eros." The second is the love of friends – "phileo." The third is true Christian love, the word "agape." This love alone is what makes a church work.

If we see God and his world, that alone won't be enough to get us to Heaven. Even if we long for these things that we see, the simple longing won't move our souls along the way. We have to actually get up and do whatever it takes to get there. Here is where we find out the price that we have to pay for our longing.

> Anyone who loves his father or mother more than me is not worthy of me; anyone who loves his son or daughter more than me is not worthy of me; and anyone who does not take his cross and follow me is not worthy of me. (Matthew 10:37-38)

"Agape" love involves a sacrifice. The reason is simple. There is too much in this world that competes for our hearts. The spiritual and the physical are at war with each other; we have to choose sides. We are constantly having to make a choice between this world or the next one. We can't have both.

> No one can serve two masters. Either he will hate the one and love the other, or he will be devoted to the one and despise the other. You cannot serve both God and Money. (Matthew 6:24)

At times that choice is going to be agonizing. Who can bear the thought of having to leave behind their family as they follow God? Yet this happens all the time, since family rarely comes to God together. Who can tear himself away from the choice temptation that the world is offering us? Yet this choice faces God's people every day, and the right road is going to be painful to the aching flesh that longs for pleasure.

The antidote for this dilemma is God's love in our hearts. Love, we learn, willingly lays down one's life for God and for his people. Jesus taught us this.

> This is how we know what love is: Jesus Christ laid down his life for us. And we ought to lay down our lives for our brothers. (1 John 3:16)

In other words, we will do *anything* – whatever it takes, whatever the price – to love God and his Kingdom, and help our brothers and sisters in the church. And because we love them, the price is not too much to pay. The only thing we will regret is that we weren't able to give more of ourselves.

This will mean beating one's body to conform it to God's standards. (1 Corinthians 9:27) This will mean dedicating my entire life, not just part of it, to God's service. (Romans 12:1) This will mean selling what I have to give to those in need. (Acts 4:34-35) This will mean putting others ahead of myself and my own wants. (Philippians 2:3-4) In fact, the more we love God and man, the less of this world we will have, and the more our lives will change – for *their* sake, not ours.

"Agape" love made the early church work. And the lack of this love that we get from God is why our modern churches aren't working at all. We don't want to give up anything or change anything in our comfortable lives. So we confess that we "love" God and man, but our actions don't show it. The requirements of love are too painful for a self-centered sinner to think about.

Nevertheless we are called to love God and man like this. Our hope is that somewhere, some church will experience this love in action by Spirit-filled believers. Love is that grace that we can't afford to do without. It's the same kind of feeling that parents have toward their children: they will do anything for the sake of their child. It's the church's only hope for survival, for accomplishing its Mission.

How does it go wrong?

I mentioned that these spiritual skills are gifts from God. They have to be, because we can't generate them on our own. There are many things that we can get better at by working on them – like knowledge – but faith and hope and love are too precious and valuable to leave to our own efforts. So, like the ability to breathe, the Spirit makes these graces automatic in our souls.

Therefore we can't escape the responsibility of these gifts by claiming that we *aren't able* to do them. That argument won't wash with God. *All* of God's people are able to believe. Why do you think Jesus was so frustrated and disappointed by his followers when they didn't believe in him? He gives us his Spirit so that we *can* believe, just as life is given to a baby so that he can live.

So, why don't Christians believe in God? Why is their hope in this world and not the next one? Why don't they love each other? The simple reason is that they've deliberately buried those gifts under a smothering weight of pleasures and wealth and comfort, and trials and suffering and afflictions. They let this world get in the way of their spiritual duty. We are given the ability to fly, yet many of us refuse to leave the ground. We go back to this world *after* we were pulled out of it – like Lot's wife.

This is called "grieving the Spirit." It happens all the time in the lives of Christians who ought to know better.

> And do not grieve the Holy Spirit of God, with whom you were sealed for the day of redemption. (Ephesians 4:30)

When the Spirit is crucifying your flesh to make you holy, why do you resist him? It's for your good! It's like refusing to take the medicine that will heal you. The Spirit is leading you to Heaven; you've been freed from this world. Why do you keep turning back to it? If you don't want God and his world, why do you keep going to church and confessing to others that you will do anything to go there? It's like Peter, who boasted that he would follow Jesus to the death – and then he denied three times that he even knew Jesus in order to save his own skin!

> You foolish Galatians! Who has bewitched you? Before your very eyes Jesus Christ was clearly portrayed as crucified. I would like to learn just one thing from you: Did you receive the Spirit by observing the Law, or by believing what you heard? Are you so foolish? After beginning with the Spirit, are you now trying to attain your goal by human effort? (Galatians 3:1-3)

This is the greatest tragedy of the modern church. We already have what it takes to succeed. All we have to do is use what the Spirit has given us. The crime is that we are still turning away from God, in spite of the fact that we've been made citizens of Heaven, and living as if we're still back in the world. If we could sit down long enough to learn what it is that is still entangling us

(Hebrews 12:1), and get rid of it once for all, we could actually make a church that works. We have the resources to succeed.

The Spirit gave us what we need to do this special work. He wouldn't be so negligent a worker as to demand things of us that we can't do. True, we couldn't do it without him; we can take no glory for ourselves. But those Heavenly powers *are* in us now. We *are* able to follow him – it's just that we don't always want to.

In other words, the children of God *are* truly saved – we just need to start acting like it.

The Spirit-led church

The typical church knows almost nothing of the leading of the Spirit, because they know so little about the Spirit and his special work. So many people are afraid to even bring up the subject, for fear of falling into excesses of hysteria that often accompany "Spirit-filled" churches.

When we won't take advantage of this important resource, we can only expect disaster, not success, for the church. We will have a bunch of independent-minded individuals doing their own thing. They won't be following the path to Heaven that the Spirit shows us, and they won't be using the resources that the Spirit puts into our hands to make that journey. And, by definition, they also won't bother doing things by the Bible, since their own will and opinions and lusts are directing their course instead of God's Spirit.

The Spirit is vital for the life of any church. In order for the ministry of the Word to succeed, the members have to be spiritual – led by the Spirit – and following the Spirit to Heaven. They have to agree to the Mission, because that's what the Spirit is committed to help us achieve. They have to have the spiritual skills necessary to cooperate with the church's ministry. You can be missing a lot of things in your church; but if the people in it don't have Christ's Spirit in them, it will never work.

The successful church *needs* Spirit-led members to accomplish its Mission. True Christians, who are driven by the Spirit, don't need any other motivation to throw themselves into the life of a church.

The Church – time to take stock

Suppose one of you wants to build a tower. Will he not first sit down and estimate the cost to see if he has enough money to complete it? (Luke 14:28)

So far we've seen that a Mission-oriented church and a goal-oriented Christian actually work together. They fit together: the church provides the very things that the serious Christian is looking for. When you have this good arrangement between the two, your church will be successful.

But if the church doesn't know what its Mission is, and doesn't provide what Christians really need in their spiritual journey toward Heaven, you've got a serious problem on your hands. Either the leadership of the church has to change things immediately to conform to the Bible's standards, or nobody would blame those sheep who leave and look for "greener pastures." It's true that people are fallible, and even church leaders may not know what they're doing. If they can learn and change, they will be able to salvage the situation and get the work of the church back on track. But if they prove to be obstinate and they refuse to cooperate with the King, he will himself come and "remove their lampstand." In other words, he won't be there anymore; he will refuse to own their cause when they won't take up his cause.

And the individual Christian ought to grow up and realize why he is in church in the first place. He's not there to be entertained, or for any number of reasons why others may go to church. He is there to reach his goal of getting ready to live with God. If he knows this, he will look for, and use, the church's resources that are designed to that end. He will tend to his spiritual growth just as much as he tends to his physical needs at home. The person who only plays at Christianity is going to be a burden to the church, not a help. He will resist the leadership's efforts to guide him in the way to Heaven, and he will try to introduce things into the life of the church that don't belong there.

Thinking ahead

People in business know that they have to sit down ahead of time and plan out what they want to do. Jumping into a business without getting things ready is just foolish; they are sure to fail. The military spends months getting ready for a major maneuver – a lot of hard work has to be done first in planning, supplies, enlistments, and training before they can go into battle and expect to win.

But for some reason, people in churches do almost no planning. The same people who would approach a worldly project with wisdom and foresight will start up a church with no thought at all about making sure the necessary elements are in place. It's as if they put their brains on idle when it comes to the church. Either it never occurred to them that this is a project that requires planning, or they think that God will accept whatever foolishness they come up with along the way.

In the following parable, Jesus warns us about being so careless when it comes to the Kingdom of God.

> Suppose one of you wants to build a tower. Will he not first sit down and estimate the cost to see if he has enough money to complete it? For if he lays the foundation and is not able to finish it, everyone who sees it will ridicule him, saying, 'This fellow began to build and was not able to finish.'

A Church for Christians – time to take stock

> Or suppose a king is about to go to war against another king. Will he not first sit down and consider whether he is able with ten thousand men to oppose the one coming against him with twenty thousand? If he is not able, he will send a delegation while the other is still a long way off and will ask for terms of peace.
>
> In the same way, any of you who does not give up everything he has cannot be my disciple. (Luke 14:28-33)

In Christ's church it is wise and responsible to sit down and count the cost. Does the church have the necessary resources in place to achieve its Mission? Does it even understand that Mission? Are the leaders willing to work for the salvation of the people of God, to feed the sheep, to be an example to the flock of what a Christian needs to be? And the members of the church – are they aware of what they're getting into? Are they prepared to submit to the ministry of the church as it prepares them to live with God? Are they ready to sacrifice their pride, their time, their families, their reputation – whatever it takes – to come under the rule of Christ?

I am aware that most churches will do at least a little bit of soul-searching along the way. There are membership classes that new members must take to join a church. Pastors are examined first before taking on the job. But what is important to realize is that the Mission is much more focused and urgent than most people are aware of. You can tell that this is true, because the leadership of many churches isn't preparing the flock according to the Mission. And members aren't working on that Mission. There seems to be a muddle about what the point of the church really is – everyone is working on different agendas.

A Church for Christians – time to take stock

The time has come to change the way you relate to church. Don't come thinking that, just because you're sitting in church, everything is OK. That's why you're there – everything is *not* OK. You're in a hospital; you're looking to the Doctor to give you something to cure you and make you whole in God's eyes. The diagnosis will be different and specific for each person, and the cure will be specific to the illness.

You've come to sit at the feet of the Wonderful Counselor who knows you and your situation better than you do. The time has come to listen to him, take seriously what he has to say to you, and follow his instructions carefully and faithfully.

The time has come to change your life. There are things that are interfering with your spiritual growth – perhaps it's the attitude you have toward church itself! Perhaps the best place to start is to bring your Bible, a pen and paper, and start studying and training right there in church. You may look strange doing that, sitting there in church like a student serious about studying, but you may be the only one there who is really taking advantage of what the church is offering people – their loss, your gain!

As Jesus said in the parable about taking stock before battle, you would do well to sit down at this point and ask yourself a serious question: am I ready to meet God? And be careful to use God's standards and requirements when you answer that question. Because many people will miss their goal of Heaven over this very issue – they used their own lower standards, they didn't attend church for what it was designed to do for them, and they will not be allowed into the presence of God.

> Enter through the narrow gate. For wide is the gate and broad is the road that leads to destruction, and many enter through it. But small is the gate and narrow the road that leads to life, and only a few find it. (Matthew 7:13-14)

Many will say to me on that day, 'Lord, Lord, did we not prophesy in your name, and in your name drive out demons and perform many miracles?' Then I will tell them plainly, 'I never knew you. Away from me, you evildoers!' (Matthew 7:22-23)

A Church for Christians – time to take stock

The Fires of Affliction

"Our God is a consuming fire"
Hebrews 12:29

Introduction

Some people learn the easy way, and some people learn the hard way. The trouble is that none of us want to learn the hard way – even if it's the best way for us to learn the lesson.

God, however, knows us better than we know ourselves. If he loves us – and he does, indeed, love his people deeply, more than we can know – then he's not going to let us continue in the kind of behavior that will destroy us. God alone knows the process that is needed to save us from our sin. He also is the only one who can justly and effectively administer the needed discipline to his children.

The easy way to learn the lessons about God, ourselves, and salvation is through the Word and Spirit, in the setting of the Church. The Bible lays it all out for us in clear and unmistakable terms. The Spirit shows us what it all means, and leads the way for us to take advantage of this truth. This is not too hard for God's children to learn and follow through on.

The problem is that we don't want to learn the easy way either. It's a willful, rebellious stubbornness (you've seen it in children, if you don't remember it in your own childhood!) that positively resists the gentle leading of our Father. When we act like that with the only One who cares for our souls, then it's time to get out the rod. He's not going to leave us in our sin and death, and he's certainly not going to let us win. It's time for us to learn the hard way.

> I will instruct you and teach you in the way you should go; I will counsel you and watch over you. Do not be like the horse or the mule, which have no

understanding but must be controlled by bit and bridle or they will not come to you. (Psalm 32:8-9)

God uses both methods to instruct his children. Unfortunately our modern church leaders, who make hardly any effort toward church discipline the easy way, particularly ignore the second method of discipline in their teaching. They have deliberately misled people into thinking that God would never be harsh with his children. That's not being fair to them at all. How will they explain the fires of affliction, trial, suffering and hardship that will inevitably come upon God's own children? Will these false prophets continue to mislead them about it – with the result that these unhappy Christians will miss the golden opportunity that affliction gives them to become righteous?

We are generally given the opportunity first to learn God's lessons the easy way. Rarely are we told, however, that if we don't learn, hard times *will* come. It's unfortunate that many people will only learn this side of God's discipline when it's too late to learn the easy way. Nevertheless, we must faithfully reveal and explain God's works to his people – particularly now, when they are struggling to understand how their Father in Heaven could allow such painful things to happen to them. God is good; God is just. The trouble that we are going through is from his hand of mercy, saving us from our sin and forming us into the image of the righteous Christ. There is nothing unfair going on here, and certainly nothing that is outside of God's immediate control.

The first thing, then, is to learn how to humble ourselves under this holy God and give him the glory and honor he deserves. If we do that under his hand of discipline, we will go a long way to turning a painful circumstance into a sweet-smelling incense to the Lord of glory.

The Fires of Affliction

> Humble yourselves, therefore, under God's mighty hand, that he may lift you up in due time. (1 Peter 5:6)

> And we know that in all things God works for the good of those who love him, who have been called according to his purpose. (Romans 8:28)

What we are going to look at in this study isn't a very pretty picture. These are words of rebuke, not comfort. It's actually addressed to those saints who, like the ancient Israelites, are "crying out to the Lord in their distress." Something has gone terribly wrong, and now they are hurting under the rod of discipline. God has much to say to them in his Word, and we're going to faithfully bring out that word of "rebuke and correction" without holding back the truth. To many, this truth will seem too harsh and out of place in the Christian scheme of things. But to those who have ears to hear, it will be – hopefully – strong medicine to bring about a permanent cure of their spiritual ills. This is the way God means it to be. The time has come for plain words.

So many people, including Christians, are hurting in this world, and they don't know why. They try to understand, but they end up saying certain things about God that are simply wrong and dishonoring to him. And yes, even Christians will complain and look for scapegoats instead of looking to their own hearts. This is not good. The sooner we come to grips with the real problem behind our trials, the sooner we will learn the lesson that our Heavenly Father is teaching us. If we resist his truth, however, we can only expect more suffering. God is no respecter of persons.

There will be those (including church leaders) who will react passionately against this idea that God would punish his people. I have no answer for them, because I don't need to answer them. The truth will be plain when God's people actually undergo such

The Fires of Affliction

suffering. The proof is in the trial itself. My only purpose here is to try to explain *why* such things happen to God's people. But you can't argue against the fact that they *do* happen.

For those who have never experienced the harsh rod of discipline under God's hand, pray that you never will. But take notes anyway, because you will gain a deeper understanding of God's ways with his children that you can use to minister to those who suffer. The Apostle Paul, who was called to endure suffering, learned his lessons well and so was able to help others in the same need.

> Praise be to the God and Father of our Lord Jesus Christ, the Father of compassion and the God of all comfort, who comforts us in all our troubles, so that we can comfort those in any trouble with the comfort we ourselves have received from God. For just as the sufferings of Christ flow over into our lives, so also through Christ our comfort overflows. If we are distressed, it is for your comfort and salvation; if we are comforted, it is for your comfort, which produces in you patient endurance of the same sufferings we suffer. And our hope for you is firm, because we know that just as you share in our sufferings, so also you share in our comfort. (2 Corinthians 1:3-7)

Disaster

Hidden sin

Sin runs deeper in our hearts and minds than we are aware of, or perhaps what we're willing to admit to. If you would ask most of us whether we are good people, we would probably answer in the affirmative. We have standards that we live by, and we think those standards ought to be acceptable to both God and man. We don't interfere with others, and our work and family and pastimes are the same kinds of things that everyone else does. As Jesus once described it –

> As it was in the days of Noah, so it will be at the coming of the Son of Man. For in the days before the flood, people were eating and drinking, marrying and giving in marriage, up to the day Noah entered the ark; and they knew nothing about what would happen until the flood came and took them all away. That is how it will be at the coming of the Son of Man. (Matthew 24:37-39)

The pagans – those who don't believe in God – are living riotous lives and don't care at all about the consequences. But people who consider themselves religious are generally behaving themselves. The average Christian, for instance, aims for living a "quiet life, minding his own business." (1 Thessalonians 4:11)

But it's not so much what the average person *does* that gets him into spiritual trouble, it's what *motivates* him. Deep in our hearts, all the sins of mankind simmer just below the surface of our daily lives. Nobody can see this sin, and we ourselves little realize what is down there until some temptation or crisis comes up and brings it to the surface. Nevertheless, those secret sins often motivate our outward actions. Rarely will someone act out of selflessness or love for others – usually we have a hidden agenda that makes us look out for Number One first.

For example, fear and greed are secret sins that focus on this world, not the next one. Out of fear we heap up treasures on earth, and not the treasures of Heaven, because we're afraid of doing without our physical comforts. Jesus exposed that motivator in his Sermon on the Mount. (Matthew 6:19-21) Greed, too, loves only the things of this world that give us pleasure and power. The common denominator is the wealth and treasure of this world – gold, houses, cars, bank accounts, clothing, property, financial security. The heart longs for these things, and is loathe to give it up. "For where your treasure is, there your heart will be also." (Matthew 6:21)

The trouble is that these two sins are buried deep in our hearts. They are unspoken motivators that lie behind much of what we do in this world. It takes the hand of God to bring them to light – and he will. Hardship makes them plain to see, and hard times prove that we are moved by less than altruistic motives. When times get rough, it turns out that we aren't as good or nice as we claimed to be. In times of trial, "Christians" as well as pagans will be revealed for what they really are.

There's another reality in human nature: we don't connect our actions with their consequences. The young don't think about consequences at all, and those who are older hope they never happen. The results of our actions, for one thing, are usually so far down the road that we don't take them seriously. Who would pass up the chance at pleasure and treasure if we could enjoy it at least for a time – even if we do have to "pay the piper" a few years later?

And when the subject of God comes up – well, we don't have time. We feel that we can safely set that subject aside for later, if ever, and continue pursuing what we want in this world. We ignore God, and for some strange reason we think that he will leave us alone too.

These and many more sins are buried deep in our hearts, like the bottom side of a hidden iceberg; they form the very foundation of our daily lives. They are deep-seated stains that are often hard to detect and almost impossible to get rid of. We are all infected with something of sin. This is the cycle of humanity – we are all like this.

As long as this situation persists, we can never be saved. God wants to cleanse our hearts and minds to the uttermost. Salvation isn't a superficial issue to him. If we would just cooperate with him and lay our hearts out before him for his spiritual cure, he would apply the balm of Christ's blood to our hearts and we would be healed. But even for many believers, this is unthinkable. They "paid their dues" when they got converted, and now they don't want to hear any more about sin. They don't like anybody, not even God, probing around inside their minds and hearts for dirt. They cover it over and forget about it just as easily and as quickly as any pagan would.

This is not acceptable to God. The very ministry of the church is designed to change us from sinner to saint, so that we can live with a holy God. What are we doing in church if we refuse to work on this problem? If we didn't know what to work on, that would be understandable; teaching in the church can correct that. But when God's people *refuse* to work on it – and act as if the problem doesn't exist – then God gets angry.

The day of disaster

Then the day for paying the penalty arrives. Having never given it a serious thought before, we learn the hard way that life is moral – it's a matter of doing the *right* thing, not the convenient or pleasurable thing. When God tells us to be perfect, that's

The Fires of Affliction – Disaster

exactly what he means. He isn't satisfied with a half-hearted Christianity. He expects us to be holy in all of our ways; he expects glory from all of us; he expects us to crucify all of our sins. He will not long tolerate an apathetic Christian.

In God's world, sinners are punished for their actions. "The wages of sin is death." (Romans 6:23) Punishment in this world, though often severe, isn't usually to the full extent of the crime, but Hell will truly round out God's justice. When punishment finally arrives (and it always does), we are shocked at how brutal it can be. *Now* we know that it wasn't worth the pleasure! But now it's too late to do anything about it.

God will not be ignored. He will not be despised. He loves his own glory more than he does all of creation. He would rather we all disappear in a roar of fire than for his glory to suffer.

> See, I have refined you, though not as silver; I have tested you in the furnace of affliction. For my own sake, for my own sake, I do this. How can I let myself be defamed? I will not yield my glory to another. (Isaiah 48:10-11)

We may not have known this about him, but the Bible shows it to us in plain pictures. God gets angry with his people when they resist him and rebel against his guidance. The children are not exempt from the Father's anger; in fact, they of all people ought to know and love God the most, and ought to be willing to obey him. When they don't, it's time to bring out the rod of discipline. And in our world, that means disaster.

Disaster is a sobering fact in our world. Again, most of us put it out of our minds during times of peace and prosperity – "It will never happen to me!" As a matter of fact, it has recurred throughout history, in all nations and races. Nobody is immune or protected from disaster. Both the good and the bad are drawn down by the floodwaters.

Let me introduce you to disaster, in case you haven't experienced it yet. It is **war** – death and destruction, pain and misery, years of brokenness and frustration and rage and anger, an indiscriminate, senseless and cruel slaughter, a destroyer of civilizations. It is *famine* – not having even the basics to live on, starvation and death and rottenness, no future for the family, no hope of relief, watching your children starve when the neighbor hoards what he can to keep himself alive. It is *plague* – the silent killer of millions that spares neither the infant nor the elderly, nor the hale nor hearty, but cuts them down in hours and fills the streets with rotting corpses, too many to count or bury. And when man starts losing control of his world under these devastating curses, he falls under the wrath of his own subjects – even the **wild animals** rebel against him.

People all through history, all around the world, have been struggling, and continue to struggle, with these grim realities. You in your comfort zone may find consolation that it has never happened to you – but it *will* happen if God so chooses. In Noah's day, the Lord destroyed the entire earth. The Israelites suffered under the harsh rule of Pharaoh. Thousands of years of tyrants and dictators have stained history with untold bloodshed and suffering. The Black Plague, it is said, killed a fourth of the human race in Europe – entire communities died from it. In our century, the World Wars brought Europe and Asia to its knees in horror and destruction. It's sobering to think that most of history is filled with appalling human suffering, all around the world. Our time of peace here in America is actually a short chapter in a long historical tragedy – it could very easily come to a sudden end. Times of peace, in the past, have always ended at some point.

The Fires of Affliction – Disaster

During disaster, the foundations are shaken. People can't continue their daily lives. Nothing is certain, not even the question of being able to eat or find clothing or stay healthy. Friends turn into enemies; the lines of death sway across the community into your house and then into your neighbor's. Nobody knows how long this will last, nobody can get away, everyone is helplessly locked into the situation with no answers. We can't predict what terrors tomorrow may bring – except we know it will get worse.

Despair and cynicism set in. Nobody cares about others. People who were once friendly and nice turn into moral monsters, willing to steal from you and even kill you to stay alive themselves. Mothers eat their children. Disaster reduces a once-powerful and intelligent and prosperous civilization to a state of barbarism, people acting in ways that you and I wouldn't have thought possible. The very air, the very ground, turns into a source of death – and terror stalks the land.

And inevitably people blame God for this. In one thing they are right – God brings disaster on men and nations. But in one crucial point they are dead wrong – they have only themselves to blame. This is *punishment* from the Creator on rebellious and sinful man. No righteous people would blame the judge for putting the criminal behind bars. Nobody in Heaven blames God for bringing the consequences of sin down on the heads of sinful humanity. And nobody would doubt that mankind deserves harsh punishment once we get a good, clear view of men's hearts – they are, as Jesus described them, tombs filled with dead men's bones. The wicked are dead souls, rotting and sending a stench into Heaven in God's nostrils. (Isaiah 65:5) He cannot stand aside and let such a moral catastrophe that they've brought upon the earth go unanswered.

Right now, Jesus is unleashing the forces of punishment on the earth. You can argue with that if you will, but the Bible shows it.

For example, the Psalms open a window into Heaven and describe his right and power to judge the earth –

>You will rule them with an iron scepter; you will dash them to pieces like pottery. (Psalm 2:9)

Revelation shows us the weapons that he has in hand to rule over rebellious subjects, sinners who will respond to nothing he has to say except harsh treatment.

>When the Lamb opened the fourth seal, I heard the voice of the fourth living creature say, "Come!" I looked, and there before me was a pale horse! Its rider was named Death, and Hades was following close behind him. They were given power over a fourth of the earth to kill by ***sword***, ***famine*** and ***plague***, and by the ***wild beasts*** of the earth. (Revelation 6:7-8)

God so punishes the whole earth because we are sinners, and he is the Judge. He created us to be righteous, and we've been anything but that. He warned us in the beginning that the "wages of sin is death," but we wouldn't listen. Now we're finding out that truth the hard way. And if someone is disposed to question God's justice in his harsh treatment of the wicked, Judgment Day will make it plain that we are, indeed, deserving of the wrath of God. Everyone will see that then, if not now.

Christians often find themselves in the middle of this war between God and man. They too are sinners, and God has to punish them of their sins as well. But their punishment is to *correct* them, to convince them that sin is not an option, that it's far better to leave that sin behind and live for God. As Ecclesiastes puts it –

>All share a common destiny – the righteous and the wicked, the good and the bad, the clean and the unclean,

those who offer sacrifices and those who do not. As it is with the good man, so with the sinner; as it is with those who take oaths, so with those who are afraid to take them. (Ecclesiastes 9:2)

If we are honest with ourselves, we would admit that we deserve everything that the wicked get. We have no goodness in ourselves. Our only hope is that Christ will change us into his image and cleanse away the same stain of guilt that marks all of humanity. God wants to see repentance and humility, especially from his own people, before he is willing to hand out spiritual blessings.

But many of us aren't so willing to admit this, not even those who attend church. We think that God wouldn't dare touch his beloved people. So, God has to resort to severe discipline at times to shake us out of our complacency and sin. We too will have to suffer what our pagan neighbors go through. There are times when even God's people must go through the fires of affliction. *Then* we will come to God in repentance and humility.

What's happening?

There are many who think that God would never put them through suffering and affliction. Unfortunately they were not taught the truth about this – God will not hesitate to put you through fiery trials for his own purposes. We have many Scriptures that teach this.

- **Job** – God brought disaster on Job, taking away everything in his life and leaving him sitting in the dust scratching his boils. He had no idea what was happening to him. He couldn't think what he had done to deserve such treatment from God's hands, though he knew his friends were wrong in their interpretation. He found out that God did it simply because he wanted to use Job as an example to Satan of a faithful servant under pressure. He learned that the Creator will do exactly as he pleases with all of his creatures, and nobody can accuse him of being unjust about it.

- **Judges** – The Israelites were supposed to live in the Promised Land under God's beneficent reign, but they fell to the flesh-pleasing temptations of the local gods instead. For this God punished them with famine, war and oppression. One would think that they would have learned their lesson, but even after they repented and God delivered them in his compassion, they went right back into their idolatry. So for centuries, in every generation, God brought disaster on his people.

- **2 Chronicles 15:5-6** – In case someone might not believe that God is behind the troubles and afflictions of nations and men, this passage spells it out clearly. "In those days it was not safe to travel about, for all the inhabitants of the lands were in great turmoil. One nation was being crushed by another and one city by another, because **God** was troubling them with every kind of distress."

- **Hebrews 12:1-13** – The writer of Hebrews encourages Christians to persevere under trials and hard times, because God is doing this to them for their own good. Would we have known this without the revelation of Scripture? Don't we naturally hate and resent hard times? But the Bible shines the light on our lives so that we can see the truth about what's really going on. Take advantage of the opportunity while God is giving it to you. Suffering brings righteousness – at least to the faithful.

- **Isaiah 5:1-7** – The prophet tells a story about God planting a vineyard (his people Israel), clearing out the stones (their sins and rebellion), planting vines (the Word of God), crushing the grapes in the vat (the difficult circumstances of life) and then waiting for the fruit that he likes to see. In other words, trials and suffering bring out the fruit of the Spirit in a good vineyard, the fruitful Christian.

- **Psalm 137** – When the Israelites repeatedly ignored God's warnings about their immorality and idolatry, he had enough – he brought the Assyrians and Babylonians into Israel and the land was destroyed. Even the Temple and the holy city Jerusalem were leveled to the ground. The survivors were dragged off into exile to Babylon; there they had plenty of time to think about their sins, as this Psalm shows us. They were in shock that God would do such a drastic and devastating thing to his own people. He does, and he will.

- **Ezekiel 6-7** – This pertains to the Exile of the Israelites to Babylon. Read here about the ruthless anger of God as he plans for his own people's destruction. There is nothing unjust here; they had hundreds of years to repent before a merciful God, and they would not. I'm sure none of them felt that they deserved this heavy-handed solution. But God makes that decision; and when he moves in wrath, there's no stopping him now.

- **Zephaniah** – The entire world got to such a point that God became disgusted with the whole thing. He vowed to destroy everybody, every nation, and start over with a righteous remnant. Even the priests and prophets of Israel were guilty!

These passages speak about what God will do with his own people; we don't have to review the widespread punishment on unbelievers, like in the time of Noah and the world-wide Flood, to see that God hates sin in all forms and will completely destroy the wicked. We have abundant examples of this in the Scriptures.

Discipline from God

The lesson here is that God will not hesitate to hurt us when we need discipline. Perhaps adults can't connect their trials with the idea of discipline. We know what it was like to be punished by our parents when we were young, but we fail to recognize another "rod of discipline" in the hard circumstances of life. And we are, for some reason, very reluctant to admit that God would be doing this to us. *First*, we usually don't think we deserve punishment (will we never grow up?), and *second*, we can't imagine why the God of love would whip us in anger.

God doesn't owe us anything. We don't deserve anything good from him. If we could see but a part of the truth, we would be amazed that he has let us live this long on his earth! We have sinned away any good treatment that he might have been obligated to show us. We have heaped the treasures of this world around us, in our fear and greed, and ignored his spiritual treasures. To make the insult sharper, we expect God to keep the physical blessings coming – as if he's duty-bound to shower us with things to fulfill our physical lusts!

The truth of the matter is that we are living in God's world on borrowed time. He's only giving us more time so that we might perhaps think about the one thing needful.

> He is patient with you, not wanting anyone to perish, but everyone to come to repentance. (2 Peter 3:9)

But if we insist on materialism, living for this world, using God as a servant to serve our lusts, living in our sin and rebellion against him, we can expect nothing good but only God's overwhelming wrath against such hardened sinners.

> If we deliberately keep on sinning after we have received the knowledge of the truth, no sacrifice for sins is left, but only a fearful expectation of judgment and of raging fire that will consume the enemies of God. (Hebrews 10:26-27)

But he doesn't have wrath against his own children – he has another form of fire. It's going to hurt, we are going to be miserable under Christ's cross, but it's designed to burn the dross from our hearts and minds and force us into Christ's image (since we rarely will do it the easy way). It's a blast furnace of affliction.

The Fires of Affliction – What's happening?

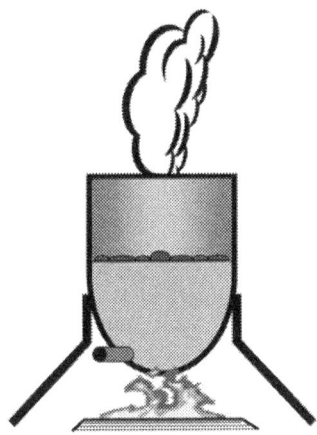

Steel makers put the iron ore in a furnace, then heat it until the iron melts out from the rock and slag so that they can pour it off into ingots. The junk – or slag – which comes floating to the top of the molten iron, is then easily scraped off the top and thrown away. In the same way, God puts the fire of affliction under our lives and refines us, separating the sins and rebellion out of our hearts and minds, so that the only thing left is the pure righteousness of Christ and the fruit of the Holy Spirit.

> For you, O God, tested us; you refined us like silver. You brought us into prison and laid burdens on our backs. You let men ride over our heads; we went through fire and water, but you brought us to a place of abundance. (Psalm 66:10-12)

The point is that it hurts – we suffer – under God's rod of discipline. There are times when he has to switch methods – from being gentle and easy, to being harsh and tough. Some of us will only learn this way.

Something about you

When affliction and trials come, it's time to take stock of our spiritual standing. If God has resorted to using discipline to get your attention, it's probably true that you've been ignoring him. Because when life is comfortable, we tend to ignore God and put spiritual issues on the back burner.

> Otherwise, when you eat and are satisfied, when you build fine houses and settle down, and when your herds and flocks grow large and your silver and gold increase and all you have is multiplied, then your heart will become proud and you will forget the LORD your God, who brought you out of Egypt, out of the land of slavery. (Deuteronomy 8:12-14)

We forget that the blessings of the world are actually side-issues to God. He can take them away from us if need be. If we've been too caught up with the blessings of this world, perhaps it's time for God to remove them – one by one, or all at once – and leave us, like Job, sitting destitute in the dust wondering what in the world happened!

Perhaps, when the Lord was telling you to focus on him, to make him your chief delight, to love him with all your heart and mind and strength, you ignored the warning and looked to other things for joy and comfort. Not that you actually *rejected* God, but you just didn't get around to taking him as seriously as the Word commanded you to. When you prioritized your day, other things took up your time – and you left God only a few minutes here and there, a stray thought when you had the extra time. Whether you knew it or not, that's an insult to God – you need him more than you think! He deserves more glory and praise than you can imagine. He continually cares for you – he gives you breath and strength to live and work in his world. Does he figure so little in your life that all you can manage is a nod in his direction once in a while? You will find him reacting in anger and destroying the comfortable nest you've built around yourself, and standing you before him to deal with him, now, in his way, in a way that will honor him.

The Fires of Affliction – What's happening?

Perhaps you have some character issues to work on. Most of us aren't alarmed at all about the spiritual state of our hearts. We knew that Jesus saves us from our sins, and we wanted him to do that – but practically speaking we have put that crisis behind us now and we're busy going on with life. Little do we know the state of our hearts! God knows – he "judges the thoughts and attitudes of the heart." (Hebrews 4:12) None of us measure up to the perfection of Christ yet. We have the capability of wrecking ourselves and others if left to ourselves. We are in no way ready to step into a holy Heaven to live with God. But until we see this, will we take time out to work on this most important of all tasks? Not until we're forced to!

So, God sends afflictions into our lives. Suddenly, as he puts the fire under us, we see all sorts of spiritual junk floating to the top of our character (for everyone to see!) that we didn't know was there: anger, greed, adultery, fear, jealousy, murderous thoughts, pride, rebellion against God, self-will, gluttony, impatience, even idolatry. What a revelation! We've been hiding these sins, these godless acts that we're still so capable of, under the veneer of a comfortable and religious life. Remove our comforts, and we suddenly become the old sinners that we thought we put behind us.

Affliction brings out our true selves. It is, again, an opportunity to see the truth about ourselves and start the difficult but necessary job of sanctifying our hearts, crucifying our flesh, so that we might be truly holy. Without the affliction we wouldn't have known the truth, nor do we want to know about it; after it, if used profitably, we will grow in righteousness.

Change the focus

If afflictions are an opportunity from God, it is of the utmost importance *not to miss the point.* It is time to change your focus.

- ***It's time to switch your attention from earth to Heaven.*** Your heart has been too much attached to this world, like Lot's wife. If you're crying like a baby over the material goods that God takes away from you, or your job or family, or even your health, then perhaps your heart isn't firmly resting on spiritual treasures yet. Jesus promised you an inheritance in Heaven – what is the loss of this world's wealth in comparison? (Matthew 6:19-21) Jesus made you a child of God and put you into his family, with whom you will live forever – would you turn away from your spiritual duties in the church for the sake of your unbelieving family, to the point that you would also suffer the penalty of Hell with them in their rebellion against God? God said that he would take care of you in all situations, like a rock in a swirling flood – do you not believe him?

    The reason we fall apart in trials and afflictions is because we aren't grounded firmly on these Heavenly realities. They aren't as real to us as the comforts of the physical world – no matter what we've been claiming in church in front of others. We don't know how to stand on them yet. Affliction, as we've seen, brings the truth out. And God *will* bring the truth out, even by making us suffer through these hard times.

    > There is nothing concealed that will not be disclosed, or hidden that will not be made known. (Luke 12:2)

> Nothing in all creation is hidden from God's sight. Everything is uncovered and laid bare before the eyes of him to whom we must give account. (Hebrews 4:13)

When all the props have been kicked out from underneath your feet, and you find yourself doing the impossible and walking on water – that is, depending on God now for everything – this strengthens your faith and gives you reason to praise God for who he is. True, we wouldn't want to go through that again, but it was good for us in the long run. The treasures of Heaven really are solid enough for us to live on! We need this physical world less than we thought.

> I know what it is to be in need, and I know what it is to have plenty. I have learned the secret of being content in any and every situation, whether well fed or hungry, whether living in plenty or in want. I can do everything through him who gives me strength. (Philippians 4:12-13)

- ***It's time to get serious about your sin.*** Sin is an insult to God. It's treason, a punishable offense. We might not think of it as such a big deal, but God positively rises up in anger over it. Little do we know his feelings about this – until he lets his anger loose in punishment.

> The wrath of God is being revealed from Heaven against all the godlessness and wickedness of men who suppress the truth by their wickedness. (Romans 1:18)

It's true that not every affliction that we might have to go through will be due to some sin in our hearts.

The Fires of Affliction – What's happening?

Sometimes it's a matter of building up our strength or faith. But few of us are like Job – "This man was blameless and upright; he feared God and shunned evil." (Job 1:1) I wouldn't start out, if I were you, with the assumption that there's nothing in your heart that needs fixing.

We each have enough sin in our hearts to destroy God's creation, as Adam did. And few of us are working on it seriously. Church nowadays is more of a celebration, a party, a social get-together where the subjects of sin and repentance are unwelcome notes to the cacophony. As we've seen, we can usually tell if the problem is sin when the affliction brings out spiritual junk in our hearts that we didn't know was there. If affliction drives us into "frustration, affliction and anger" (Ecclesiastes 5:17) then our "faith" doesn't mean much. "If you falter in times of trouble, how small is your strength!" (Proverbs 24:10) Our hearts are steeped in sin, we've been ignoring it, and now God deems it time to bring everything out into the open and change a hypocrite to a saint.

- *It's time to humble yourself.* When trials come your way, now is not the time to be in denial. It's not someone else's fault; you can't start looking around for a scapegoat to blame for your troubles – including God.

    A man's own folly ruins his life, yet his heart rages against the LORD. (Proverbs 19:3)

    The reason God is putting you through this is to change you. You are not what he wants you to be. It's time to come to him empty-handed, setting aside hard feelings, ready to examine your heart and life for *anything* that offends him. If you are as perfect as Christ then you have the right to come to him and demand an accounting from him (which even Christ didn't do in his affliction!). Short of that, you can assume that the perfect and holy God has decided that you need more work.

> Search me, O God, and know my heart; test me and know my anxious thoughts. See if there is any offensive way in me, and lead me in the way everlasting. (Psalm 139:23-24)

What could the trouble be? It might be that you don't love God enough. It might be that you've been entertaining some sin in your mind and heart. It might be that you have too much attachment to this world instead of the next world. It might be that you offend your neighbor – you're not as nice a person as you thought. It could be any number of things. The solution is to open the Bible, go to God in prayer, and implore him to make you into the Christian that you claim to be. Not just to escape further trials, but over a genuine grief that you are not yet made into the image of Christ, and that you've offended your Father in Heaven and driven him to chastise you like this.

Humility – God likes that. He hates the heart of pride, the person who arrogantly claims that he is no sinner, that there's nothing wrong with *his* faith. God longs to see willing servants, like the tax collector at the Temple, confessing their great need of God's salvation continuously, fully, expectantly.

Humility

Let's go back to that last point and expand on it. Humility is such a crucial characteristic of God's children if they want to get anywhere with him. It was said of Moses that he was "a very humble man, more humble than anyone else on the face of the earth." (Numbers 12:3) What this means is that he came before God with the right attitude – an attitude that opened up the mercy and treasures of God. Pride, on the other hand, slams those doors shut.

- Humility starts with a confession of our true nature. We dare not come before God as a "good" person. We are sinners – and until that truth grips our minds so that it dictates the very way we deal with God, we will get nothing from him. It's a fact, so we may as well face it and deal with it.

- We are also only creatures, the dust of the earth and not capable of taking care of ourselves. As the Scripture says, we can't even keep ourselves from dying! God faithfully feeds us every day – he gives us the very sustenance we need to live. Humility acknowledges the hand of God in virtually every aspect of our lives. If it weren't for God's constant care and faithfulness, we would have nothing.

- Humility knows that we deserve nothing from God. If he is good to us, it's simply because he wants to be – not because he owes us anything. We are living on his mercy to sinners. We dare not come to him demanding, or expecting, anything apart from his sheer will and pleasure – if we do, we will get nothing from him.

The Fires of Affliction – What's happening?

Clothe yourself with humility and you will go far with God. First of all, you will realize that you've been running your life for too long. You've been pursuing the vain treasures and pleasures of this world; it's been pretty much your only agenda. And all you have to show for it is failure, emptiness, frustration, having gotten nowhere for all your efforts. Your ways don't work – it's time to admit that. Perhaps, if your sights are set on only the fleeting happiness in this world, you can achieve that for a time. But being a believer, your hopes are in the next world, not this one. What have you done to prepare for that? What reason would God have for letting you into his Kingdom, in light of your past deeds?

> For we must all appear before the judgment seat of Christ, that each one may receive what is due him for the things done while in the body, whether good or bad. (2 Corinthians 5:10)

Secondly, humility will cause you to come to God like a child. A child believes what his father tells him. A child follows his father and emulates him. A child hangs his head with shame when the father disapproves of his actions. A child loves his father, and trusts him completely. A child obeys his father without questioning him. These character traits are the perfect picture of what a Christian needs to be with God. This is why Jesus told us to become like children.

> I tell you the truth, unless you change and become like little children, you will never enter the kingdom of Heaven. Therefore, whoever humbles himself like this child is the greatest in the kingdom of Heaven. (Matthew 18:3-4)

The problem is that we are too much like adults – self-willed, independent, proud, hard-hearted, not willing to take a rebuke.

That gets us nowhere with God. *We have to change this*, in order to claim the name "Christian."

Humility will also drive you to God to accept *whatever* he gives you. The affliction is never enjoyable; we hate pain and hardship. We tend to take God himself to task, in fact, by expecting him to remove hardship out of our lives – and when he does, then we'll love him again. No – *you have to learn to love the hand that beats you.* This is your Father in Heaven correcting you; this cross that he laid on you is for your good. It is literally your salvation. Watch Paul as he learned this lesson for himself:

> To keep me from becoming conceited because of these surpassingly great revelations, there was given me a thorn in my flesh, a messenger of Satan, to torment me. Three times I pleaded with the Lord to take it away from me. But he said to me, "My grace is sufficient for you, for my power is made perfect in weakness." Therefore I will boast all the more gladly about my weaknesses, so that Christ's power may rest on me. That is why, for Christ's sake, I delight in weaknesses, in insults, in hardships, in persecutions, in difficulties. For when I am weak, then I am strong. (2 Corinthians 12:7-10)

Will you learn?

As we've seen, adults don't think that they need to go through punishment anymore. They left that behind when they were children. All they want now are the good things of life – they certainly don't think that God is going to start disciplining them as if they were still children.

They are wrong. People with this kind of attitude are headed for a rude awakening. God can and will discipline his children, and the more obstinate ones are going to hurt more for it. It's for their own good. If God would do nothing with them – which is what they want – then he doesn't have any plans to save them.

> If you are not disciplined (and everyone undergoes discipline), then you are illegitimate children and not true sons. (Hebrews 12:8)

So, when affliction strikes you, don't miss the lesson in it. God is talking to you. It's time to humble yourself and admit that you need more work spiritually. You may not know why you're going through this hardship, but God does – and he will tell you if you have the right attitude with him. A wrong attitude will only get more of a beating, since the brutish and senseless will only understand a beating. "A wise son heeds his father's instruction, but a mocker does not listen to rebuke." (Proverbs 13:1) Wisdom seeks the right answers – and welcomes them.

Anybody who obstinately refuses to change and learn under affliction is positioning himself for Hell. God has no patience with fools – particularly wicked, rebellious fools. See Proverbs on this.

Affliction is the opportunity to grow in grace, to know Christ deeper, to see the glory of God, to cut the ties to this wretched world, to long for the treasures of Heaven, to train your heart to be a servant of the King. What Christian would refuse this opportunity, painful though it be, if it results in eternal life?

> Let us fix our eyes on Jesus, the author and perfecter of our faith, who for the joy set before him endured the cross, scorning its shame, and sat down at the right hand of the throne of God. (Hebrews 12:2)

> Therefore we do not lose heart. Though outwardly we are wasting away, yet inwardly we are being renewed day by day. For our light and momentary

troubles are achieving for us an eternal glory that far outweighs them all. So we fix our eyes not on what is seen, but on what is unseen. For what is seen is temporary, but what is unseen is eternal. (2 Corinthians 4:16-18)

Critical issues

Affliction is usually due to the fact that we haven't been taking God seriously. He has to hit us with the rod of discipline to get our attention, and make us willing to change. Many of us refuse to learn the easy way; so God resorts to pain – the language we all understand. Yes, it hurts, and we didn't think that our loving Father would hurt us deliberately. But it isn't going to kill us – just save us.

> He who spares the rod hates his son, but he who loves him is careful to discipline him. (Proverbs 13:24)

> Folly is bound up in the heart of a child, but the rod of discipline will drive it far from him. (Proverbs 22:15)

> Do not withhold discipline from a child; if you punish him with the rod, he will not die. (Proverbs 23:13)

Whether you fall under one or more of the following categories, the point is that your thinking, your feelings, your actions, your entire lifestyle has to change to conform to God's expectations of you. You are doing something wrong in his eyes; you are not yet what he expects of you. And evidently you haven't been listening to his gentle rebukes in his Word, or through other believers. Learn the lesson, and the trial that you're suffering under right now will turn out to your long-lasting benefit.

Turn to God

God is the supreme being. All the rest of us are created beings, existing at his pleasure, depending on his good will for even the basics of life. He didn't need us before he made us, and he can easily get rid of all of us if that was his will and it wouldn't affect his nature in the least.

This requires a certain attitude from us – and it isn't pride. As we've already seen, humility is the characteristic that will get you somewhere with God. The thought that this God wants you, and is willing to put up with you until he can change you into his image of righteousness, ought to stagger your mind. There is no reason in yourself for this kind of attention from him.

One of the main reasons for trials and afflictions is that we have forgotten about God, in the midst of our prosperity and worldly affairs.

> When you have eaten and are satisfied, praise the LORD your God for the good land he has given you. Be careful that you do not forget the LORD your God, failing to observe his commands, his laws and his decrees that I am giving you this day. (Deuteronomy 8:10-11)

We are totally dependent on God for everything, whether we acknowledge it or not. Yet God gets almost no glory for what he does in this world – everyone claims credit for being wise and strong and clever and good, when really it's God working behind the scenes setting up history the way he wants it to go. (It seems, however, that God gets the blame for everything!) If we have anything to glory over, it was first a gift from God to us. He is the source of all good things.

> For who makes you different from anyone else? What do you have that you did not receive? And if you did receive it, why do you boast as though you did not? (1 Corinthians 4:7)

The goal of the Christian is that God might become his *all in all*.

> When he has done this, then the Son himself will be made subject to him who put everything under him, so that God may be all in all. (1 Corinthians 15:28)

God is the source of all good. We know wisdom in him alone; we know strength in him alone; we know peace and joy and justice in him alone. As we touch him, as we get closer to him, these realities become strong meat to us – we would rather live with this God than settle for the empty shadows of the things that this world offers us.

Our modern definitions of love lack the passion that God wants to see in our hearts. Jesus told us how to love God.

> Love the Lord your God with all your heart and with all your soul and with all your mind. (Matthew 22:37)

This means that we set aside prime time to look for and find God. We spend time with him. We love the things he gives us; we despise the world's vain promises. God becomes a priority for us, not just an empty name. Our one goal is to know more and more about God, whatever it takes – because he is so rich and good to know.

> Now this is eternal life: that they may know you, the only true God, and Jesus Christ, whom you have sent. (John 17:3)

> I want to know Christ and the power of his resurrection and the fellowship of sharing in his sufferings, becoming like him in his death, and so, somehow, to attain to the resurrection from the dead. (Philippians 3:10-11)

> How lovely is your dwelling place, O LORD Almighty! My soul yearns, even faints, for the courts of the LORD; my heart and my flesh cry out for the living God. (Psalm 84:1-2)

You have to understand, of course, that even though we might bring ourselves to a high level of longing for God, he will control the relationship. He's the wise and just one. He may decide that the first thing you need to learn is obedience to the King – due to your rebellious and stubborn heart. We don't dictate anything to God, nor will we fool him with false zeal. A true love for God is willing to lie at his feet and accept whatever God wills for him – even if it means the cross. Hardship from God's hand is a blessing, and medicine for the soul. That's the kind of attitude that God wants in us, if he's going to share his life with us. He's no fool. "Do not be deceived: God cannot be mocked." (Galatians 6:7)

Our duty is to learn as much about God as we can. The Bible, of course, is the textbook. It's the complete revelation of everything we need to know about God. The Lord will guide us through the lessons – at the pace he knows we need to take, in the order we need to learn it. But he's looking for willing students who genuinely want to know and glorify him with their lives.

This is a far cry from our modern tendency to do as little as possible in our Christianity. The church has not always been so. We modern Christians are lazy, we expect things immediately or we lose interest, we see no need in delving deeply in intellectual pursuits (unless it's an interesting hobby!). We therefore suffer when we bring this attitude into the church. We say things about God that are absurd; it's obvious that we are making things up about him, because such notions didn't come from the Bible. And our ignorance of him has a high price – this is the biggest factor behind the cults growing at such an alarming rate in our day and leading ignorant souls to Hell. Only with a full knowledge of the truth of God will the saying from Paul be true of us –

> Then we will no longer be infants, tossed back and forth by the waves, and blown here and there by every wind of teaching and by the cunning and craftiness of men in their deceitful scheming. (Ephesians 4:14)

The state of your soul

Your soul is the most precious thing that you own. It's a real shame to watch people take such care over their physical lives – their health, their comforts, their appearance – and give no thought at all to the stinking, rotting reality in their hearts.

Your soul needs life. Your soul needs food and drink from Heaven to survive. Your soul needs the light of Heaven to avoid the pitfalls of this world. Your soul needs proper clothing before you can come into God's presence in his Heavenly court. You have desperate spiritual needs that have to be tended to daily, whether you know it or not.

> You say, 'I am rich; I have acquired wealth and do not need a thing.' But you do not realize that you are wretched, pitiful, poor, blind and naked. I counsel you to buy from me gold refined in the fire, so you can become rich; and white clothes to wear, so you can cover your shameful nakedness; and salve to put on your eyes, so you can see. (Revelation 3:17-18)

Probably because the spiritual world is invisible, and the soul is hidden away inside us, is the reason we forget about its condition. We don't worry about what we can't see. We are more concerned with the pressing, immediate concerns of our physical existence. Then, when certain circumstances come up that require a healthy spiritual response, we find that we have neither strength nor understanding on how to handle it. Our souls are crippled – ignored over the years, starved to the point of death, unable to deal with the affairs of the Kingdom of God.

So what have we gained by ignoring the condition of our souls? Why did we think that such a focused attention on this world – its pleasures and treasures – would be what we need? It isn't!

> What good is it for a man to gain the whole world, yet forfeit his soul? Or what can a man give in exchange for his soul? (Mark 8:36-37)

Jesus told a story about a man who paid no attention to the needs of his soul; in fact, unknown to him, spiritual disaster was right around the corner waiting while he was making plans to make life here more comfortable!

> The ground of a certain rich man produced a good crop. He thought to himself, 'What shall I do? I have no place to store my crops.' Then he said, 'This is what I'll do. I will tear down my barns and build bigger ones, and there I will store all my grain and my goods. And I'll say to myself, "You have plenty of good things laid up for many years. Take life easy; eat, drink and be merry."' But God said to him, 'You fool! This very night your life will be demanded from you. Then who will get what you have prepared for yourself?' This is how it will be with anyone who

stores up things for himself but is not rich toward God. (Luke 12:16-21)

The time has come to pay attention to the state of your soul. You've been ignoring it too long. You need spiritual meat and drink to make it strong and healthy. You need rebuke and discipline to get it in line with God's will. You need fellowship with other saints – fellowship around Christ – to form a proper spiritual world view, and join your comrades in arms against the enemy of our souls. There is much to do here to lose your spiritual fat and get you in shape to "run the race."

> Do you not know that in a race all the runners run, but only one gets the prize? Run in such a way as to get the prize. Everyone who competes in the games goes into strict training. They do it to get a crown that will not last; but we do it to get a crown that will last forever. Therefore I do not run like a man running aimlessly; I do not fight like a man beating the air. No, I beat my body and make it my slave so that after I have preached to others, I myself will not be disqualified for the prize. (1 Corinthians 9:27)

If you lose your soul, you've lost everything. Only your soul will survive the dissolution of this world. Nothing in this world is going to survive Judgment Day except *you*. What will you say if you show up before God's judgment seat spiritually destitute, having no profit to show the Master?

The goal of your salvation is nothing less than perfect righteousness. Remember, however, that the idea is not for you to try to become righteous on your own. You must take on Christ's perfect righteousness – and that happens by following the leading of the Spirit (as he leads you away from this world and toward Heaven), living by faith, learning about God through his Word, resisting the enemy of your soul, and many other things. If you accomplish nothing else in this life – even if you are a nobody in the world's eyes, poor and despised – you will have lost nothing, and gained everything, if you tend to your soul, first and foremost.

> And everyone who has left houses or brothers or sisters or father or mother or children or fields for my sake will receive a hundred times as much and will inherit eternal life. (Matthew 19:29)

The wise Christian will use all means at his disposal to improve his spiritual condition. This includes the vast resources that God has made available to him in the Church setting, where the gifts of the Spirit are specially designed to prepare a soul for life with God in Heaven.

When can we rest from our labors? When we are finally standing firmly on the foundation of Christ, in all ways, so that we can survive any disaster.

> Therefore everyone who hears these words of mine and puts them into practice is like a wise man who built his house on the rock. The rain came down, the streams rose, and the winds blew and beat against that house; yet it did not fall, because it had its foundation on the rock. (Matthew 7:24-25)

Discipline

Discipline is not the narrow idea that most people have about it. Some organizations understand exactly what discipline is – like the military. It's a world view, it's a way of approaching life, it's a system designed to help us get the job done. It's not just punishment for committing a crime.

The average Christian is far from being disciplined! This is in fact one of the main reasons that God has to lay hardships on us. If the child would have obeyed his parents, he wouldn't have been punished. But it takes the right attitude, and years of training, to do God's will as he expects of us. And *that* is *not* happening in today's churches.

We are an independent lot. We don't like anybody telling us what to do, we don't like admitting that we need to improve, we don't like having to measure up to standards, we don't like to put forth effort on things that don't interest us, and we will leave on the slightest offence. If our army was like that, we would have been overrun by our enemies long ago. That is, in fact, why our spiritual enemies are having a field day in our churches.

The ***first*** issue about discipline is to establish the authority structure. We are not the authority! God is our authority. When we became Christians, we acknowledged Jesus as Lord and Master. Why do we then treat him as if he's our servant, and we're unhappy with his performance when he doesn't give us, or do for us, what we want from him? There can be no discipline with an attitude like that.

Second, God has issued our orders and we must learn them and obey them – without question, immediately. We are not here to do our will but his will. He will not tolerate our opinions or willfulness or any arguments. He expects our obedience, or we will suffer the consequences. It's all written out and explained for us in his Word.

Third, discipline means training. Christianity is not a day-long seminar with coffee and donuts. It means spending long hours over the textbook, praying that God would give us the skills to do our duty, using these things we've learned at every opportunity, looking for weaknesses and fixing those, and training even more. It means never relaxing at your post, always alert and ready to jump into the task. It means going over this material and skills until the Master himself is satisfied that you have got it.

Fourth, the purpose of discipline is to present a united, strong front against the enemy – and winning the battle. The way the church is today, we can't possibly win our battles – and as a matter of fact we aren't. The world is winning, and our country as well as the church has turned into a dark realm of wickedness and death. It's time we learned how to use the weapons of God against the forces of darkness – and may God give us courage and perseverance to fight this good fight of faith. Only then can we turn things around and enjoy God's blessings in our church and society.

The Family of God

We all have priorities, and for many of us our priorities are job, family, entertainment, and perhaps (if we have some time left) God and church.

That's exactly backwards. And if God has to bring out the rod and correct your wrong notion of what's a priority, he will. The priority is God first, church second, everything else third.

I know this won't go down well for many who love, for instance, their families more than their brothers and sisters in the church. As we've seen already, God has a different view on the subject of family than we do. But it bears repeating, because for some, the lesson has to be forcefully made. Much hardship in the lives of believers comes from the reluctance to switch families.

> Anyone who loves his father or mother more than me is not worthy of me; anyone who loves his son or daughter more than me is not worthy of me. (Matthew 10:37)

In fact, in the places that I've found in the Gospels where Jesus talks about our families, Jesus was, in all ten passages, either neutral toward the idea of family or cynical about it. These modern churches that have "family oriented ministries" didn't get that idea from the Bible.

The reason for this is not because Jesus doesn't like families. He whole-heartedly supports the idea of a family being strong around God and spiritual realities. It's just that he knows that's rarely going to happen.

> Do not suppose that I have come to bring peace to the earth. I did not come to bring peace, but a sword. For I have come to turn 'a man against his father, a daughter against her mother, a daughter-in-law against her mother-in-law' – a man's enemies will be the members of his own household. (Matthew 10:34-36)

God doesn't draw eternal lines around earthly families any more. That was the rule during the time of the Israelites, but not now. In our day we have a new family – the Church.

> For whoever does the will of my Father in Heaven is my brother and sister and mother. (Matthew 12:50)

It's true, we're supposed to take care of our families. It's true, Paul talks about family members and their obligations to each other. But that's not our problem now. We've swung to an extreme of focusing on our families to the exclusion of our spiritual brothers and sisters. I have seen Christians in overwhelming need in the midst of those who could have, and *should* have, helped them – but refused to.

> What good is it, my brothers, if a man claims to have faith but has no deeds? Can such faith save him? Suppose a brother or sister is without clothes and daily

food. If one of you says to him, "Go, I wish you well; keep warm and well fed," but does nothing about his physical needs, what good is it? (James 2:14-16)

I have seen people stab each other in the back in a church, and willingly destroy the work of God and bring the ministry to needy souls to a complete halt – and then walk away from their crime against the church as if they had done nothing wrong.

> If anyone says, "I love God," yet hates his brother, he is a liar. For anyone who does not love his brother, whom he has seen, cannot love God, whom he has not seen. (1 John 4:20)

In Heaven there will be no more families – no marriage, no having children, no grandparenting. All that is nice when it works well, but it rarely works well. Instead God is drawing a line around a new family – the children of God, who have one Father and an Elder Brother. You will find that, once you arrive in Heaven (if you do!) your earthly family will probably not be there with you. Those are the statistics, anyway.

> Enter through the narrow gate. For wide is the gate and broad is the road that leads to destruction, and many enter through it. But small is the gate and narrow the road that leads to life, and only a few find it. (Matthew 7:13-14)

The only way you can solve that disaster is by getting your earthly family members saved and into the Body of Christ. Fathers, mothers, brothers and sisters, children and cousins – they are *children of the devil* (as you once were – see John 8:44; Ephesians 2:1-3), and your spiritual enemies until they switch sides and become Christians. Like Pilgrim in John Bunyan's **Pilgrim's Progress**, you must be willing to leave them behind if they won't come with you as you follow Christ.

The Fires of Affliction – Critical Issues

This awareness of the importance of God's family was a hallmark of the early church. It was said of them that –

> There were no needy persons among them. For from time to time those who owned lands or houses sold them, brought the money from the sales and put it at the Apostles' feet, and it was distributed to anyone as he had need. (Acts 4:34)

So much for Junior's inheritance! That money went to someone in the church who had need of it. The modern rich American sweats blood at the very thought of doing that! How ironic – we are, of all the nations of history, the best able to do such deeds of love, and yet we are the most reluctant to do so. Even for those whom we profess to "love" in the Lord.

But that is what love really means – putting yourself out, doing without if necessary, going through hardship if need be, so that your brother and sister in Christ might find relief and experience the hand of God blessing them through you.

Perhaps you didn't know this – God prefers to do his work through man. He rarely reaches down and does some miracle directly to solve a problem. *You* are his servant. *You* are the means through which he will build his Church, his eternal Kingdom, his family. If you haven't been taking this high-priority project of his seriously, then no wonder he's getting your attention and making your life difficult for you!

> This is what the LORD Almighty says: "Give careful thought to your ways. Go up into the mountains and bring down timber and build the house, so that I may take pleasure in it and be honored," says the LORD.

"You expected much, but see, it turned out to be little. What you brought home, I blew away. Why?" declares the LORD Almighty. "Because of my house, which remains a ruin, while each of you is busy with his own house. Therefore, because of you the heavens have withheld their dew and the earth its crops. I called for a drought on the fields and the mountains, on the grain, the new wine, the oil and whatever the ground produces, on men and cattle, and on the labor of your hands." (Haggai 1:7-11)

Prayer

Most people will pray at one time or another. Usually it's when they get in trouble and they want God to rescue them. But you can't tell whether this kind of prayer is really genuine – it may be that, if God would deliver them as they ask, they would just go right back into their sin and ignore him again.

> When you ask, you do not receive, because you ask with wrong motives, that you may spend what you get on your pleasures. (James 4:3)

Prayer is one of the least practiced, and therefore least understood, of our spiritual duties. People who spend a great deal of time preparing a Bible lesson will give no thought to the contents of a prayer until the time comes to pray. For some reason we pray whatever might be in our heads at the time, and we think that God will be satisfied with such a prayer.

He isn't. And if we've been praying in such a slip-shod and careless manner, he will let us know by not sending answers when we need them. He's going to step back and let us struggle with problems we can't solve – without his help.

Approaching God requires a great deal of thought and preparation. God is a King, and should be approached as such. Only a fool will barge into a king's throne room and blab whatever comes into his head at the moment. He will be a royal embarrassment in front of the court. And that's precisely what we look like, in God's throne room in the Temple of Heaven, surrounded by thousands of angels who surely cringe when we blunder into God's presence and pretend to tell the King how to run his own Kingdom!

The Old Testament can provide a great deal of help here. The laws concerning the Temple teach us about the holiness of God, how to approach him with humility and sacrifices, what kinds of things to ask for, what are important issues to him, and so on. It sheds a lot of light on the process.

This means, then, that you have some learning to do – you have to learn how to pray. If you don't want to learn and change your ways, that's up to you – but don't expect any answers from the King! But if you want God to hear you, it's time to learn the rules and get good at talking to the Lord of glory.

David, for example, was good at prayer. So was Nehemiah, and Moses, and Daniel, and Jesus, and Paul, and the other great saints of Scripture. Learn to pray as they did, and you will get answers. You must be willing to spend a lot of time on this, and change some bad habits of yours, and "set your eyes on things above" – all of which are necessary to become an effective prayer warrior.

To hear people pray nowadays, I can't imagine them or the church getting spiritually strong on such ignorance. We are not here to line our worldly nests! God's Kingdom matters are on his heart – are they your concern too? The enemy is destroying the holy city – where are the warriors who can push him back in battle? The whole secret to eternal life is to know God – do we pray so that this might happen? The one thing preventing us from knowing him, and going there to Heaven to live with him, is our sin – are our prayers aiming at those sins like spiritual cannons and blasting them into oblivion?

It's no sin to be an infant. The problem comes when that infant turns 20 and is still acting like an infant. Hopefully all the years behind your profession of being a Christian has made you spiritually strong and wise – like an adult. Do your prayers reflect this? The church needs you to be mature, and God has been training you to be mature. If you're not, God may feel that you need a beating to make you grow up and take his Kingdom seriously.

The Bible

We've been mentioning the need to know the Bible all along, but it deserves a special mention.

Most adults are done with learning. They graduated from school, they have a job and family, and they don't want to learn anymore. They feel that whatever they know now is all that they need to know. Unfortunately this attitude pervades the church – the American church, at any rate. You just can't get people to come out to Bible study anymore. They don't even take a Bible to the church service. They own a Bible – but don't expect them to *study* it!

The ignorance of the Bible is profound in our generation. Surely we fulfill the words of the prophet:

> You stumble day and night, and the prophets stumble with you. So I will destroy your mother – my people are destroyed from lack of knowledge. Because you have rejected knowledge, I also reject you as my

priests; because you have ignored the Law of your God, I also will ignore your children. (Hosea 4:5-6)

Notice an alarming thing in this passage. Not only are the people ignorant about God, but the leaders are too! Ignorance of God runs across the entire spectrum of the church. You would think that the leaders would know about the Bible – being seminary-trained – but according to their sermons they seem to have little concept of the "deeper truths" (1 Timothy 3:9) of the Christian faith. The Old Testament is a particular problem here; most churches even pride themselves on being "New Testament churches." There's a practical reason for this: they simply do not understand the Old Testament. It's too confusing, they don't see the connection between it and the New Testament – so they ignore it.

This is the purpose of the Bible: it reveals God to us, from first to last. In its light we will see not only the true God – in all of his ways, works, character, names, and attributes – but we will also see ourselves in light of him – that is, that we are in great need of him. The Bible shines the light of Heaven on everything around us so that we can understand what's really going on. Now we know why we need to worship God. Now we know why this world is so dangerous to our souls. Now we know why Jesus is such a fitting answer to our problems. All this comes to light in the Bible.

For this reason the Bible is critical for our spiritual well-being. As long as we are in the dark about everything we will be an unwitting target for our enemies. Shining the light not only chases them away, it shows us a sure-footed path to life and safety. We see the resources we need to survive in this dark, wicked world. We learn the rules for relating to God – our former enemy, now our Father.

Let's go one step further: unless you open your Bible and *learn*, you cannot be saved. You will lose this battle of life. Only those who have faith will please God (Hebrews 11:6), and faith only comes by reading and studying the Bible. (Romans 10:17)

The church in particular gives us an excellent opportunity to study the Bible. The people who can teach it are there, and the gifts of the Spirit are there to make sure that the children get the truth from Heaven. Christ provides just the right materials from Heaven, and the skills and labor to carry it through, in the setting of his church.

Psalm 1 tells us how to approach the Bible – not superficially, not in just a few minutes when you get a chance, but with a great deal of thought.

> But his delight is in the Law of the LORD, and on
> his Law he ***meditates*** day and night. (Psalm 1:2)

Meditation requires time and effort. It means digging out the meaning, not only in the passage that you're studying but in other passages that shed more light on it. It means taking this material to God in prayer and pleading for light on it. It means staying with a passage until you understand what God wants you to know from it – and how it fits into the bigger picture that is starting to form in your head from your on-going study of the Bible.

A witness

There's been some confusion about the idea of "witnessing" in today's church. Young believers are often given a Bible and sent out into the street to "witness" to others – in other words, to preach the Gospel of Christ to unbelievers and lead them to the Lord.

This is in fact one of the spiritual gifts that Paul lists in Ephesians 4:11 – it's the work of an *evangelist*. And, as Paul reminds us, we do *not* all have this gift. Only some do. The reason is because evangelism requires a good deal of training and knowledge so that some weirdo doesn't successfully back you to the wall and prove to you that you don't know what you're doing when confronting capable pagans.

We are all, however, called to be *witnesses*. A "witness" is someone who has seen or heard something that others might be interested in, or need to know. In a courtroom, the judge may have a difficult time deciding whether the accused really did commit the crime. Evidence can be read in more than one way, and we certainly can't just take the word of the accuser or the accused as final. But when a witness testifies that he saw the accused do the crime, the case is closed – it's a powerful proof of the event and it decides the issue immediately.

Christians are different from proponents of other religions. The pagans can only talk *about* their gods, because (since their gods don't exist!) they've never seen their gods or heard them. Their information is hearsay only – they can rely only on long generations of traditions and philosophies that pretend to describe a god that never was. Christians, however, have each seen their God – it's a requirement for getting into the faith. Each believer knows that Jesus is real because he has and still does meet with Jesus through the Word, through prayer, and through the Spirit. "I ***know*** whom I have believed." (2 Timothy 1:12)

This is a devastating yet simple proof against unbelief that God has provided for us, and it's actually our first line of offense against the enemy. There's no argument against it. How can anybody deny someone's testimony of what they have seen and heard from their God except by calling them a liar?

Being a witness is both a privilege and a duty. It's a *privilege* because we are one of the honored few who have met God and lived through it – Jesus changed us, fixed us, and raised us up into the presence of God. Now we sit and reign with Jesus at God's right hand. Even the angels are staggered at such a turn of events. We know things about God – and experience them – that no other creature has ever known, nor would they dare to think it possible for them. We talk to our God daily, and he talks to us.

The *duty* lies in the fact that we were made for a purpose – we were made to glorify God. All of creation brings glory to God, but we Christians have another message that no part of creation can claim. We were once mortal enemies of God, but now we are his children because of his infinite mercy and grace. We have experienced the full love of God in Christ Jesus. That's what we are called to witness to. Sinners need to hear this, so that they might also come into the light. Angels need to hear this, so that they might wonder at the unfathomable love of God to the undeserving.

In light of the fact that we have this privilege and duty, do you suppose that perhaps we have lost our focus when we are so immersed in the things of this world that we put our spiritual treasure on the back burner – as if the things of God are of less importance than the cares and pleasures of this life? Do you think that we don't appreciate what God has done for us when we complain about the little hardships that we have to endure in this life? How in the world can a redeemed child of God, heir of righteousness, born for the throne of God's universe, filled with the Spirit, receiver of all the promises of God – how can this saint honestly complain that things aren't going in a way that suits him?!

If we have so lost sight of our calling as to fall to such a low level in our spiritual walk, then it's time for some discipline. Hopefully when we've lost these things that we cherish more than

God, then we will turn to our true inheritance and find our joy in that – and be the witnesses once again that we were created to be. God *really is* our only love and joy. And we will be happy to tell others that.

The fear of the Lord

You may be offended with the idea that God would be so demanding of his subjects, and harsh toward those who disobey him. But the Scripture teaches us that God will not be trifled with. His honor and glory come before our comfort.

> The fear of the LORD is the beginning of knowledge, but fools despise wisdom and discipline. (Proverbs 1:7)

If you have severe problems in your life, you may want to start with humbling yourself before this God who does *all things well*. The problem may be you; it's certainly not him. It will only hurt matters by blaming God, or insisting that God would never resort to pain and hardship to train his wayward children – "Why would God allow this to happen!" For us, pain is unacceptable; to him, however, it's a tool to shape us into his image.

> But I have stilled and quieted my soul; like a weaned child with its mother, like a weaned child is my soul within me. (Psalm 131:2)

The time has come to quit playing games with God and take him seriously. When he feels that you've sufficiently humbled yourself under his hand of discipline, then he will relent and show you his mercy and grace.

> Humble yourselves, therefore, under God's mighty hand, that he may lift you up in due time. (1 Peter 5:6)

Summary

War – plague – famine – chaos – death and destruction. The Babylonians swarmed over Judah and Jerusalem, killing and destroying, and hauling treasure and survivors back to Babylon.

Habakkuk, the prophet, couldn't believe that God would allow these pagans to bring disaster on his holy people. His prayer was the cry of a saint in distress, struggling to understand how such a disaster could happen under God's benevolent rule. "Why do you tolerate wrong?" (Habakkuk 1:3)

The reason, he found out, is that God was using these pagans to punish his people. When the Israelites had angered God yet once again with their idolatry and immorality, he drew the line – the time had come for harsh treatment. He called the feared Babylonians to come and destroy his beloved people.

It wasn't something that God wanted to do. They forced his hand. He had sent prophet after prophet over hundreds of years to turn them around, to bring them to repentance of their sins and rebellion. They wouldn't listen. Well, God is a just God – not even his own people are going to get away with sin.

> For it is time for judgment to begin with the family of God; and if it begins with us, what will the outcome be for those who do not obey the gospel of God? (1 Peter 4:17)

The mercy is that this isn't the last word we will get from God. The pagans will suffer and die, and that's the end of their story. But believers suffer and learn – and *change*. We have this opportunity to at least learn the hard way (since we failed to learn the easy way!) and enter into the door of life. The wise will not despise this opportunity.

> And you have forgotten that word of encouragement that addresses you as sons: "My son, do not make light of the Lord's discipline, and do not lose heart when he rebukes you, because the Lord disciplines those he loves, and he punishes everyone he accepts as a son."
>
> Endure hardship as discipline; God is treating you as sons. For what son is not disciplined by his father? If you are not disciplined (and everyone undergoes discipline), then you are illegitimate children and not true sons. Moreover, we have all had human fathers who disciplined us and we respected them for it. How much more should we submit to the Father of our spirits and live! Our fathers disciplined us for a little while as they thought best; but God disciplines us for our good, that we may share in his holiness.
>
> No discipline seems pleasant at the time, but painful. Later on, however, it produces a harvest of righteousness and peace for those who have been trained by it. Therefore, strengthen your feeble arms and weak knees. "Make level paths for your feet," so that the lame may not be disabled, but rather healed. (*Hebrews 12:5-13*)

www.ingramcontent.com/pod-product-compliance
Lightning Source LLC
Chambersburg PA
CBHW032039150426
43194CB00006B/352

9780615145709